JOHN RALSTON SAUL founded the LaFontaine-Baldwin Symposium in 1999 and is its chair. He has had a growing impact on political thought in many countries. His writings include *Voltaire's Bastards*, *The Unconscious Civilization* (the Massey Lectures) and, most recently, *The Collapse of Globalism*. In his essays, he explores the human struggle for personal and social balance, and he aims at developing a new humanism through what he calls "responsible individualism." He was president of the Canadian Centre of International PEN from 1990 to 1992 and is now its honourary chair, and was named by *The Utne Reader* as one of the "100 Visionaries of the World" in 1995. Recently, he became the co-chair of the new Institute for Canadian Citizenship. Mr Saul's honours include being named a Chevalier de l'Ordre des Arts et des Lettres of France (1996) and a Companion of the Order of Canada (1999), as well as being awarded the Governor General's Literary Award for *The Unconscious Civilization* (1996) and the Pablo Neruda International Medal of Honour (2004).

ALAIN DUBUC is one of Quebec's most prominent journalists and public intellectuals. Trained as an economist at the University of Montreal, Mr. Dubuc first became a business reporter for *La Presse* in 1976. He went on to become the chief editorialist at *La Presse* and then president and editor at *Le Soleil.* Under his leadership, the pages of these newspapers became must-reads for those concerned with the interplay of economics, power politics and political philosophy. Mr. Dubuc is the author of *As Simple As Economics* and has hosted the Télé-Quebec television show *Money Matters.* He now works as a columnist for both *La Presse* and *Le Soleil.*

GEORGES ERASMUS has made a lifelong contribution to the welfare and community of Canada's Aboriginal peoples. From 1976 to 1983 he served as the president of the Indian Brotherhood of Northwest Territories/Dene Nation. He was subsequently elected as national chief of the Assembly of First Nations in 1985, then re-elected for a second term in 1988. In 1996, Mr. Erasmus co-chaired the groundbreaking Royal Commission on Aboriginal Peoples. He currently resides in Yellowknife, N.W.T., and leads the Aboriginal Healing Foundation as president and chairman. He is also the chief negotiator for the Deh Cho First Nations.

 BEVERLEY McLACHLIN has had a distinguished career as a lawyer and is one of Canada's leading judicial figures. Educated at the University of Alberta, Ms. McLachlin began her career in law in 1969 in Edmonton and went on to practise and teach law in Vancouver. She served on the B.C. Supreme Court and the B.C. Court of Appeal before her appointment to the Supreme Court of Canada in 1989. On January 7, 2000, she was appointed chief justice of Canada. She is the first woman in Canada to be named to this position.

 DAVID MALOUF is one of Australia's most celebrated authors and public intellectuals. His published work runs to nineteen volumes, spanning such diverse genres as poetry, fiction and opera librettos. Mr. Malouf's modern and classic *Remembering Babylon* was short-listed for the Booker Prize in 1993. His books include *Johnno*, *An Imaginary Life*, *Harland's Half Acre*, *The Great World* and, most recently, *Dream Stuff.* He is a graduate of the University of Queensland and has taught in Europe and Australia. He currently works as a full-time author and lives in Sydney, Australia.

 LOUISE ARBOUR is one of the world's most renowned judicial figures. She has earned an international reputation for speaking out on human rights across the globe. Ms. Arbour received her law degree in 1970, subsequently assuming the positions of associate professor and associate dean at York University's Osgoode Hall Law School. In 1987, she was appointed to the Supreme Court of Ontario and then, in 1990, to the Court of Appeal for Ontario. In 1996, she undertook her most public role when she became chief prosecutor for the International Criminal Tribunals for the former Yugoslavia and Rwanda. After three years as prosecutor, Ms. Arbour resigned to take up an appointment at the Supreme Court of Canada. On July 1, 2004, she became the United Nations high commissioner for human rights.

DIA LOGUE ON DEMO CRACY

THE LAFONTAINE-
BALDWIN LECTURES
2000–2005

WITH A FOREWORD BY **JOHN RALSTON SAUL**

LOUISE ARBOUR
ALAIN DUBUC
GEORGES ERASMUS
DAVID MALOUF
BEVERLEY MCLACHLIN
JOHN RALSTON SAUL

EDITED BY RUDYARD GRIFFITHS

PENGUIN
CANADA

PENGUIN CANADA

Published by the Penguin Group

Penguin Group (Canada), 90 Eglinton Avenue East, Suite 700, Toronto, Ontario, Canada M4P 2Y3 (a division of Pearson Penguin Canada Inc.)

Penguin Group (USA) Inc., 375 Hudson Street, New York, New York 10014, U.S.A.

Penguin Books Ltd, 80 Strand, London WC2R 0RL, England

Penguin Ireland, 25 St Stephen's Green, Dublin 2, Ireland (a division of Penguin Books Ltd)

Penguin Group (Australia), 250 Camberwell Road, Camberwell, Victoria 3124, Australia (a division of Pearson Australia Group Pty Ltd)

Penguin Books India Pvt Ltd, 11 Community Centre, Panchsheel Park, New Delhi – 110 017, India

Penguin Group (NZ), cnr Airborne and Rosedale Roads, Albany, Auckland 1310, New Zealand (a division of Pearson New Zealand Ltd)

Penguin Books (South Africa) (Pty) Ltd, 24 Sturdee Avenue, Rosebank, Johannesburg 2196, South Africa

Penguin Books Ltd, Registered Offices: 80 Strand, London WC2R 0RL, England

First published 2006

(WEB) 10 9 8 7 6 5 4 3 2 1

Copyright © The Dominion Institute, 2002, 2006
Foreword copyright © John Ralston Saul, 2006

Manufactured in Canada.

LIBRARY AND ARCHIVES CANADA CATALOGUING IN PUBLICATION

Dialogue on democracy : the Lafontaine Baldwin lectures, 2000–2005 / with a preface by John Ralston Saul ; edited by Rudyard Griffiths.

ISBN 0-14-305428-7

1. Representative government and representation—Canada. 2. Nationalism—Canada.
3. Native peoples—Canada. 4. Canada—Politics and government—1993–.
I. Griffiths, Rudyard   II. Title.

FC60.D43 2006   971.07   C2005-907195-8

Visit the Penguin Group (Canada) website at **www.penguin.ca**

Special and corporate bulk purchase rates available; please see **www.penguin.ca/corporatesales** or call 1-800-399-6858, ext. 477 or 474.

To Louis-Hippolyte LaFontaine and Robert Baldwin, two architects of Canadian democracy

∾ CONTENTS

∼ FOREWORD

History often deals with our intentions the way a turbulent spring river deals with flotsam and jetsam.

In the second half of the eighteenth century, an Enlightenment idea of the nation-state emerged. It was abstract and based on principles that were said to be rational. History carried this concept forward into the socially turbulent, nationalist nineteenth century, during which the whole concept of the nation-state was cannibalized into one of *people and place as revealed truth*. For the next two centuries, Western civilization frantically abandoned the broader humanist idea of multiple identities. This was replaced with a belief in sacred borders. God and destiny had apparently ordained that these borders should divide us, for our own good so that we could flower, each as a pure people with monolithic destinies.

All over the West political mechanisms were put in place to eliminate the complexities of co-existing multiple races, languages, religions and, in particular, multiple mythologies. Local differences were increasingly denigrated. In various nation-states, central ministries of education had schoolchildren on their feet at the same moment everywhere within their particular borders reciting the same texts.

This nationalism produced a wide range of positive outcomes. There was an explosion in both egalitarian education and public services. Clean water and sewer systems virtually rid our cities of rampant deadly diseases. Fairer law enforcement and more accessible courts made a broad public life possible for many. Unfortunately, this same nationalism also encouraged and unleashed that eternal human weakness known as fear. Worse still, it focused much of that fear on the unknown *other* — that human who does not fit into our monolithic definition of ourselves. And so racism and other forms of national myopia were increasingly normalized through the nineteenth century until in the twentieth they produced unprecedented levels of violence.

Canada was a peculiar player and non-player through all of this. We had our fair share of Protestant–Catholic riots, as the Orange Order and the Ultramontanes imported their European prejudices into Canada's complexity. The situation began to spin out of control as early as the 1840s when the British government deliberately blocked Robert Baldwin's law aimed at stopping in its tracks the Orange Order's spread of racist evil. Empires almost always play the minorities in their colonies off against each other. Occasionally this may have the happy outcome of protecting a fragile minority. But even then the method used is aimed at aborting the development of healthy local societal relationships. And that is, of course, the conscious imperial intent.

But the responsibility of Canadians was also great. You have only to look at the flowering of anti-Aboriginal policies after Confederation and the insidious growth of anti-Semitism.

There was a long list of other expressions of classic negative nationalism in Canada. We embraced precisely the same sort of exclusionary policies being put in place in varying degrees everywhere in the West.

The LaFontaine-Baldwin Symposium is an attempt not to draw on the idea that people and place are a revealed truth. There was always another Canada. Not a country of revealed truth, but one truer to the complexity of its place and its peoples. This was a profoundly non-monolithic idea of the nation-state, running at counter-current to the dominant Western monolithic approach. What's more, I believe that this was a constant and determining undercurrent, which made and continues to make the country what it is: non-monolithic because it continues to be built on its triangular foundation of English, French and Aboriginal cultures; a triangle strengthened by the continuing return in presence and power of the First Nations. What comes with this is the ability to take pleasure in a complexity of multiple loyalties; the ability to see regional tensions as often in a positive light as a negative one; and a growing linguistic sophistication. The continual waves of immigrants who inherit the best and worst of what they find, then find themselves rolling into the evolution of the whole. This complexity has been rolling on for more than four centuries without the forces of monolithic purity ever approaching positions of real power. Constantly rolling and yet doing so in a way that is an unbroken form of stability.

Since 1848, our democracy has been constant, flawed, yet capable of improving itself. Our historic mechanism for this improvement has two faces. The first is the non-monolithic undercurrent which does create a sense of social agility — of

positive tension. Where does it come from? We can only specu-
late. Perhaps the basis was the absence of a clear majority for any
one group, combined with the difficulty of surviving here. The
other mechanism grew out of this non-monolithic tradition. It
was and remains the conscious intellectual expression of public
policy structures put in place from 1848 on by the reform movements of Louis-Hippolyte LaFontaine and Robert Baldwin in
the Canadas and by Joseph Howe in Nova Scotia. During the
turbulent years from 1848 to 1851, the foundations of modern
Canada were institutionalized, enshrining the notion of the
public good. From justice systems to public education and public
universities, from a professional civil service to the beginnings of
labour law, from government involvement in cutting-edge private-
sector programs to the removal of European-style class structures,
more than a hundred key initiatives set us on our current track.

That we can trace the practical ethical foundations of our
society back to those three years around 1850 matters because it
gives us a solid reference point. Those successful reform movements, with their clear verbal and written expressions of a just
society, can be a constant mirror for our efforts today. Eighteen
hundred and forty-eight gives us a trajectory — a line through
our history — along which we can judge our failures and our
successes and our need to move on in order to strengthen our
egalitarian nature.

And that is what these first six lectures are all about. I
launched the series with a lecture laying out the Great Ministry's
contribution between 1848 and 1851 and its relationship to
today's realities such as chronic homelessness, for example. Alain
Dubuc then sent a shot across the anglophone bow, forcing us
to face up to our unconscious nationalism. Georges Erasmus
drew all of us into the single great continuum of our society —

the evolving role of First Peoples and the implications for all Canadians. Beverley McLachlin reminded us of how cutting-edge our approach to living with differences is, yet how fragile it is and how much conscious effort is needed to accommodate this approach. David Malouf drew us into our mirror — Australia — the other country whose experience most resembles ours; whose successes and failures carry messages for Canadians. Here is an accurate reflection devoid of the deformed colonial images we often get from Britain, France and the United States. Louise Arbour then rounded out this first series by engaging in the sort of ethical and practical projection that LaFontaine, Baldwin and Howe would have recognized as true to their project. She pushed us towards a new, expanded understanding of rights and therefore of justice by focusing on the right to basic well-being.

In other words, here are six propositions about the nature of modern Canada. And they are enveloped by an informal, wide-ranging conversation among the six participants on all these issues.

What then is the book's aim? It is an attempt by people who don't need to take risks with ideas to do exactly that. Why are they such willing participants? Because this sort of debate about ideas and ethics and citizenship is exactly what a society like ours needs to keep us linked to our foundations, yet constantly moving forward. Stability requires the intellectual agility to keep on re-inventing yourself. That is the true nature of continuity.

Canada is one of the oldest continuous democracies, the second-oldest continuous federation, arguably the oldest continuous democratic federation. After all, the American Senate, as powerful as the president, often more powerful, was still appointed, not elected, until just before World War I.

And yet, in spite of almost 160 years of unbroken democratic experience, we somehow have difficulty seeing ourselves in this way. We rarely imagine ourselves as an old, stable society, let alone as the intellectual construct we are; one that has emerged from a muscular shaping of ideas. It is in good part thanks to those ideas that we have manoeuvred our way through repeated crises, making mistakes along the way, sometimes awful mistakes, but never fatal ones.

Political ambition and a strange incapacity to remember the reality of our experiences has led to a curious and constant insistence on talking about Canada as if it were new. I would call this an embarrassing and naïve insistence on our newness. We may continually add new elements to our society as we roll forward, but we are an old, stable civilization and highly experienced. And that is one of our key strengths.

There is one other related point. While we have survived our errors, all of our close friends in the Americas and in Europe have committed the sort of unforgiving mistakes that then dragged them down into civil war, and led to sustained internal violence, coups, dictatorships and profound political breakdown. The conclusion to be drawn is simple.

Since 1848, our American and European allies have slipped into these catastrophes, some several times. We have often come dangerously close to the precipice, but we have so far managed to draw back from it. To have avoided the worst suggests a certain talent for living with our complexity. But this has only been possible because we have assumed the intrinsically experimental and cutting-edge nature of our society in a conscious and intellectual way. We have acted, having thought and debated. This is why thinkers, historians and activists like Margaret Conrad, Anne Golden, Rudyard Griffiths, Gerry Friesen,

Jocelyn Létourneau, Émile Martel and Bob Rae have made these lectures happen and have led the sustained public debates that emerge from them. They believe, as we do, that public policy grows out of ideas and debate.

John Ralston Saul
January 2006

∼ ACKNOWLEDGEMENTS

This book, and the continuing success of the LaFontaine-Baldwin Symposium as it enters its seventh year, would not have been possible without the support of an outstanding group of public-minded individuals and organizations. The Dominion Institute and John Ralston Saul would like to thank TD Bank Financial Group for its generous multi-year support of the symposium; Diane Turbide and David Davidar of Penguin Group (Canada); Michael A. Levine, counsel to the symposium; the entire LaFontaine-Baldwin Advisory Board; and our media partners Boréal, *La Presse, Maclean's* and the Canadian Broadcasting Corporation. We would also like to acknowledge the efforts of Alison Faulknor of the Dominion Institute, who played a key role in assembling this compilation.

For more information on the symposium, please visit **www.lafontaine-baldwin.com**.

∽ INTRODUCTION

When Canadians think about the founding of our democracy, we usually conjure up the textbook image of Confederation: men in waistcoats poring over mounds of parchment in high-windowed rooms. Beneath this benign pictogram lies a pernicious myth.

We have come to believe that the creation of our democratic values and institutions was a purely pragmatic exercise, a series of jurisdictional horse trades between French and English Canada, between Mother England and its colonies. The birth of Canadian democracy, or so the story goes, was not the result of bold vision or charismatic leadership. Rather, the coming of democracy to the Canadas was supposedly the by-product of colonial elites' pursuit of economic gain and personal ambition through political union.

The convention that political expediency and self-interest defined Canada's journey from colonial oligarchy to democratic community does a great disservice to our public memory and present-day civic discourse.

At one moment, the belief that our democracy sprang from an act of political pragmatism erases the fact that our democratic culture was the product of profound choices among competing visions of the public good. Far more violent and intolerant futures than the present we inhabit could have flowed out of Canada's political founding. This inclination to see the coming of democracy to Canada as an inevitable and non-ideological process also devalues our present-day attitudes about civil society. It leads us to assume that our democratic culture is somehow an imperfect copy of the ideas and institutions that sprang from the great political experiment in America.

However, there is a different way to think about the origins of our democratic culture, one that gives us a deep appreciation of the political dynamism and intellectual originality of our democracy. This interpretation traces the genesis of Canadian democracy back to the rough-and-tumble decade of the 1840s and the actions and ideas of two great but largely forgotten heroes: Louis-Hippolyte LaFontaine and Robert Baldwin.

LaFontaine and Baldwin were political reformers whose lives were defined by the Rebellions of 1837. Both men believed passionately in the idea of responsible government — the principle that Canadians should be governed by a cabinet responsible to the elected legislature and not the executive fiat of the governor general. For Louis LaFontaine, the survival of French culture and the cause of liberty meant travelling to Britain to plead for reform, only to be imprisoned on his return to Quebec. Robert Baldwin, a prominent reform figure in pre-Rebellion administrations and the fountainhead of responsible government, condemned the armed insurrection in Upper Canada, but, in the Rebellion's aftermath, he found himself a social outcast, half a lifetime's thinking about political reform discredited by his peers.

Yet just ten years later, LaFontaine and Baldwin would lead Canada's first democratic government. As collaborators, they would give life to many of the institutions and values that we now associate with the democratic character of Canadian society. In the space of a decade they would also create a new political culture for Canada, one capable of subsuming divisions of language, ethnicity and religion in an overarching notion of the public good.

The genius of LaFontaine and Baldwin was the consistently principled, inclusive and democratic stance they took towards the series of social and political crises that defined the 1840s. In the wake of the 1837 Rebellions, the reform movement and French Canada were faced with the fallout from Lord Durham's disastrous 1837 report. On Durham's recommendation, the British Colonial Office had merged Upper and Lower Canada into one political unit represented by a single Parliament. The Colonial Office's long-term goal was the gradual assimilation of French-Canadian culture by the English-speaking majority. The immediate political intent of union was the dilution of the reform elements in both provinces in Parliament, where the Protestant English minority in Quebec would combine with the Tory element in Upper Canada to form a powerful conservative majority.

As the 1840s got underway, the use of the French language was banned in the new legislature. During the elections for the first Parliament, the governor general aided and abetted sectarian violence against French and Anglo reformers. Wholesale political patronage was used to entrench Tory opponents of responsible government in key administrative positions. Democratic reform seemed an all but impossible goal.

What was the reaction of LaFontaine and Baldwin to these reversals, which followed so quickly on the humiliations of

1837? Both understood that the path to democracy lay in a policy of active collaboration between French and Anglo reformers. This collaboration would not consist of a return to rebellion. Rather, they would exploit the democratic potential of the new assembly to form a powerful French-Anglo reform majority. By winning legitimacy in the eyes of the public, this reform majority could wrestle executive authority over domestic affairs from the governor general.

Baldwin quickly put the reform agenda into action with two bold steps. First, he resigned from the Executive Council on the principle of responsibility when the governor general failed to heed his advice that reformers, including LaFontaine, be brought into the new administration. Next, he arranged for LaFontaine to run in a by-election in one of the two Toronto-area ridings that had elected Baldwin himself to Parliament. After losing his own seat to sectarian thuggery in Lower Canada, the leader of French Canada was triumphantly returned to Parliament by a Protestant, Upper Canadian constituency. This gesture cemented the French-Anglo reform partnership for the decade to come. It would also echo through the course of Canadian history, from the famous Macdonald-Cartier alliance all the way to the 1963 Royal Commission on Bilingualism and Biculturalism.

The hands-on task of bringing about responsible government fell to LaFontaine. Ever the brilliant parliamentary tactician, he used Baldwin's theories of responsible government to fight a protracted and public battle against the executive authority of the governors general. But his real contribution to Canadian democracy was in neutralizing the secessionist movement in Quebec, which saw co-operation with the Anglo reformers as a threat to the survival of French culture. Again and again, LaFontaine held together the French reform coalition against a radical republican movement, which sought political autonomy through annexation to the United States or outright revolt. Had LaFontaine lost his reform majority in and outside Parliament, the reform movement would have been stillborn in Upper Canada and Quebec set on the course to a second civil insurrection.

Democracy finally came to the Province of Canada in the winter of 1848. A landslide election victory for French and Anglo reformers and the arrival of a new liberal governor general made responsible government a fait accompli. It became fact when LaFontaine and Baldwin were called upon to form a new Executive Council and draw, as they saw fit, from the ranks of their reform party. LaFontaine and Baldwin were no doubt pleased that victory had been won not by adopting their opponents' tactics of gerrymandering and intimidation but by winning broad public support for the reform project and its vision of a shared democratic future for French and Anglo Canada. In ten short years, majority attitudes in the Province had undergone a seismic shift.

Of the reforms put into effect under the "Great Reform Ministry," three initiatives underline the vision of LaFontaine and Baldwin for a common democratic future that endures to the present day. The use of French in the legislature and for government business was championed. Government was brought closer to the people through the establishment of locally elected, self-governing municipal councils. And the multi-decade fight over the relationship of organized religion to higher education was brought to an end with the creation of the University of Toronto as a publicly funded, non-sectarian institution.

The responsible government of Baldwin and LaFontaine faced its greatest test when it dealt with the destruction of property that had occurred during the Rebellions. In the aftermath of the uprisings, the new legislature approved equivalent indemnities for Upper and Lower Canada. Yet it later became apparent that the damages in Lower Canada were twice as great. To nail the lid tight on the last major issue fuelling separatism there, LaFontaine felt bound to pass legislation providing adequate compensation for French Canadians. In doing so, he tapped into long-standing Tory anger towards the rebels and rekindled their fears, especially in Montreal, about what the French reform majority would do with its new-found power. In the midst of riot and bedlam in Parliament and in the streets of Montreal, the governor general held to the principle of responsible government and made the bill law. That night, the Parliament of the Province of Canada was burned to the ground by an angry Tory mob.

In the aftermath of the burning of Parliament, the democratic culture fostered by LaFontaine and Baldwin triumphed. Rather than sending troops against the rioters or executing their ringleaders — as was happening all over Europe as the revolutions of 1848 were violently suppressed — elite and public opinion rallied around the reform values of political accommodation and social tolerance. And in the absence of a martial response, the spectre of the Rebellions that haunted French and Anglo relations was exorcised. It was almost as if the anger that had rotted at the core of both communities since 1837 was itself consumed in the blaze of Parliament.

The story of LaFontaine and Baldwin and their fight for responsible government opens up a whole new way of looking at the achievement of democracy in Canada. Instead of economic pragmatism or personal ambition, Canadian democracy flowed out of the political imagination and ethical force of LaFontaine and Baldwin's reform movement. The two men created the foundations for a democratic, egalitarian society where citizens could participate fully regardless of language or creed.

Their real genius, though, was to be able to imagine, in the dark days of the early 1840s, an inclusive and democratic future for Canada, and then lead a Province rife with sectarian division to this collective goal. Their patient adherence to an ethic of accommodation over withdrawal — their invention of a true politics of inclusion — saved their generation from the sectionalism that leads all too often to civil war. LaFontaine and Baldwin ultimately gave Canadians a distinct theory and style for the practice of democracy, one that has allowed us over 150 years to embrace successive waves of economic, demographic and technological change.

Discovering what is unique in the Canadian democratic experience and re-imagining a common democratic future for Canada are the twin goals of the LaFontaine-Baldwin lecture series. Established by His Excellency John Ralston Saul in 2000, the annual LaFontaine-Baldwin lecture has quickly evolved into the pre-eminent national forum for exploring the historical antecedents and future trajectory of our democracy.

This volume contains the first six years of LaFontaine-Baldwin Lectures by John Ralston Saul, Alain Dubuc, Georges Erasmus, Beverley McLachlin, David Malouf and Louise Arbour. Each lecture stands by itself as a cogent analysis of the challenges and opportunities associated with the practice of democracy in Canada today. Together, they provide a powerful triangular framework — a fusion of the Anglo, French and

Aboriginal perspectives — that propels us beyond the confines of our time and place to imagine, in the spirit of LaFontaine and Baldwin, the kind of democracy we think fairness and justice demands.

Rudyard Griffiths, Editor
January 2006

DIA
LOGUE
ON
DEMO
CRACY

John Ralston Saul

〜 INAUGURAL LAFONTAINE-BALDWIN LECTURE

Royal Ontario Museum
Toronto, Ontario
Thursday, March 23, 2000

Why devote so much effort to the past, when tonight, in this city, there are four to five thousand homeless, a thousand of them children, half of them families with children?

Perhaps the answer lies in our reaction to these numbers: a little shudder of horror or surprise and then they roll off our back. The next time we hear them, well, we've already heard them. What else is new? And they remain, stubbornly, numbers, not people with lives.

So I add, what is the past when set against the thirty thousand who will experience homelessness over the next twelve months in Toronto, remembering that only 17 percent of them are chronically homeless? The vast majority, therefore, are caught on the precarious ledge of poverty for dozens of reasons, and from time to time are shoved off or slip off and then desperately crawl back up again. How many are on the ledge? Some eighty thousand in this city.

Do you feel those numbers intruding on you, crashing up against your sense of well-being and then rolling off, down to the floor? Tomorrow there will be more numbers from different sources on different subjects — an export number up or down; a dollar number up or down; inflation, unemployment, waiting times in emergency wards, a tax statistic, a student-debt calculation. Each will cause a sensation, positive, negative, a small catharsis, of the headline or police-drama sort.

These numbers have become our modern form of gossip; they are the *People* magazine of public policy. Somehow, the lives that lie behind the drama cannot be integrated into our consciousness in a long-term way. Instead there is a sense of immobility. "That's the way things are." "There isn't the money." It is as if, seen from within the complexity of our systems, it is impossible to identify the relationship between responsibility and action.

Curiously enough, these same surging waves of numbers also create an impression of urgency — almost a mental state of siege. And yet this is an unusual urgency because it is not attached to any practical sense of the obligation to deal with the cause. It is as if we are addicted to the emotion of urgency for its own sake, and so rush on, from fast emotion to fast emotion, in a directionless manner.

Which brings me back to the false, Manichaean question: if today is filled with an urgent reality, is not time spent in the past self-indulgent?

But the past is not the past. It is the context. The past — memory — is one of the most powerful, practical tools available to a civilized democracy. There is a phrase that has been used over the centuries by various writers in various countries: History is an unbroken line from the past through the present into the future. It reminds us of our successes and failures, of their context; it warns us, encourages us. Without memory we are a society suffering from advanced Alzheimer's, tackling each day like a baby with its finger stuck out before the flames.

Each time I hear one of those speeches that invoke Canada, the new country, I am reminded of our self-imposed Alzheimer's. New? It is more than four centuries since the Aboriginals, francophones and anglophones began their complex intercourse in this place. We are the second- or third-oldest continuous democracy in the world — 152 years without civil war or coup d'état. Look around at our allies. Compare.

Each of us, through birth or immigration, brings something new to this experience. We add. We change. But for better and for worse, we do not erase. Only ideological dictatorships erase.

With the past we can see trajectories through into the future — both catastrophic and creative projections. The central trajectory of the modern Canadian democratic society has its foundations in the great reform alliance of Louis LaFontaine and Robert Baldwin; and indeed in that of Joseph Howe, which brought democracy to Nova Scotia a month before LaFontaine formed his responsible government on March 1848.

The words *responsible government* so underplay the importance of the event that we miss its real meaning: the responsibility is that of the government to the people's representatives; 1848 was the moment when the very legitimacy of our society was switched from the colonial elites to the citizens.

Of course it was a flawed democracy. Women without the vote. Not even all men. But in the context of that time the suffrage was large compared with what existed in other countries. The high levels of land ownership — you needed land to survive — meant the electorate that chose Howe, LaFontaine, Baldwin was dominated by poor, largely illiterate farmers. They had a sophisticated idea of their own ambitions and responsibilities.

What gives meaning to the arrival of democracy is not the event itself; not the abstract action of voting; certainly not the power-oriented idea of majorities. What made this the key to our past, present and future was the context that surrounded the event.

The reformers sought democracy because they imagined a certain kind of society. Ils avaient un projet de société. If you take today's apparently abstract "situation" of poverty — of child poverty, for example — and place it in the context of the intent of 1848, it takes on real meaning. Meaning as to what the concept of democracy is intended to include in this society.

Joseph Howe:

The only questions I ask myself are, What is right? What is just? What is for the public good?

I would press any ministry of which I was a member to take the initiative ... in every noble enterprise, to be in advance of the social, political and industrial energies which we have undertaken to lead.

Robert Baldwin warned of "the consequences of that reckless disregard of the first principles of [democracy and justice] which, if left unchecked, can lead but to widespread social disorganization with all its fearful consequences."

And from Louis LaFontaine, in what for me is the cornerstone document of modern Canada — his Address to the

Electors of Terrebonne in 1840 — these words, which cannot be repeated enough:

> Pour nous empêcher d'en jouir, il faudrait détruire l'égalité sociale qui forme le caractère distinctif tant de la population du Haut-Canada que de celle du Bas-Canada. Car cette égalité sociale doit nécessairement amener notre liberté politique…. Il ne peut exister au Canada aucune caste privilégiée en dehors et au-dessus de la masse de ses habitants.

> *The only way that the authorities can prevent us from succeeding is by destroying the social equality that is the distinctive characteristic as much of the populations of Upper Canada as of Lower Canada. This social equality must necessarily bring our political liberty…. No privileged caste can exist in Canada beyond and above the mass of its inhabitants.*

Is this romanticism? Of course LaFontaine knew there would always be richer and poorer. But he — they — were inventing the idea of a profoundly middle-class society, in which that middle class would be as inclusive as possible. And they were centring it not on the European idea of the self-interested bourgeoisie but on a rather peculiar new idea of what Baldwin called "the happy conduct of public affairs." Happy — in the eighteenth-century sense — meaning the fulfillment of the common weal.

What sounds romantic today was to many infuriating. The quasi-totality of the Canadian elites did everything they could to deny political power to the democrats — or call them the humanists or the reformers or the advocates of happiness, that is, of the public good. And for almost eight years the reformers refused the blandishments of power. Or rather they wouldn't trade their principles for power. By today's standards of *real-politik* they were stubborn and weak. They lacked ego and ambition. They stuck to their principles.

We often say that compromise is a Canadian virtue, that compromise has got us through the difficult situation of our complex population, complex internal geography and complex foreign relations. It was the reform leadership of 150 years ago that developed this idea of compromise. But their idea had nothing to do with our contemporary use of the word to describe self-interested negotiations through which each of the stakeholders gets a piece of the pie. Nothing to do with shared selfishness bought at the expense of the public weal.

Their compromise was based upon confidence in the people and an understanding of the principles at stake. Baldwin spoke of "that forbearance, moderation and firmness on the part of the people which, so long as it compromises no great principle, affords the best assurance of the possession of fitness for the exercise of political power."

And so, when the citizens did at last give them power, it was based upon the solid foundations of a shared understanding of the operating principles of the society. Over the next three years — a mere three years — they changed, reformed, revolutionized in every direction. They put in place the foundations of modern Canada.

This hall is surrounded by Robert Baldwin's university. It was consciously designed by him to remove higher education from the hands of the colonial elites — that is, the religious, financial and social elites. The intent was to create a broadly based, disinterested public education, and it became the model for Canada's higher learning. In other words, he put in place the idea of universities as necessarily public institutions.

It's just worth remembering today, when the very ideal of the independent public university is in question, that Baldwin's reform faced violent attacks. There were, as there still are, those who thought a less public system would permit opportunities for personal profit and influence. Among them, Bishop Strachan — whose Trinity College lies a few metres from here — argued that such a university would "place all forms of error on an equality with truth, by patronizing equally … an unlimited number of sects, whose doctrines are absolutely irreconcilable…. [S]uch a fatal departure from all that is good is without a parallel in the history of the world."

The beginning of a fully funded, universal public school system was also put in place. They understood that this was — and this remains — the key to our functioning democracy. They extended the principles of responsible government into the towns, villages and townships. This creation of municipal democracy involved a great decentralization of power and of responsibility, a second democratic revolution meant to bring legitimacy so close to the people that no authority could remove it. They reorganized the judicial system, including key legislation on trial by jury. They decentralized the trial system so that justice was available to the majority of the population for whom a trip to town was an economic burden. Both in Canada and in Nova Scotia they opened up the railway system, beginning our transportation revolution. They put through our equivalent of an anti–rotten borough bill. They removed primogeniture, a self-inflicted blow, given Baldwin's own interests as a man of property. It was a government in the best tradition of the Republic of Dubrovnik, which had lasted a thousand years.

Over the door of that city state's Great Council were the words "Forget your business and attend to the public one."

There were dozens of other basic changes that even today decide the shape of our society. But let me come back to a key point: the real meaning of that word *compromise*. Not trade-offs, but moderation in the light of basic principles. When the Château Clique and their allies came out into the streets of Montreal on the night of April 25, 1849, and burned down the Parliament of Canada, the government responded with moderation. Everywhere else in the West, governments automatically responded to such situations with rifles and cannon. The Executive Council — the cabinet — met on the twenty-seventh in the midst of the ongoing disorder and ratified a report that would explain their policy. It stated that "the proper mode of preserving order is by strengthening the Civil Authorities." And that the "Council deprecate the employment of the Military to suppress such disturbances …"

It was one of those perfectly existential moments. Here was a fragile half colony / half country, which already had two languages, as well as many ethnic groups and religions — without even taking into account the Aboriginal role as a founding member of the society. In nineteenth-century terms it was a powder keg. The government's response would cause this place either to slip down the European/American road towards impossible oppositions, outright violence and a centralized monolithic model, or the ministers would have to discover another way.

Somehow, LaFontaine and Baldwin reached down into their own ethics and imaginations and decided upon an original and much criticized response. The imperial government in London, for example, was furious that the streets had not been cleared with volleys of rifle fire. The great Western historian W. L. Morton has put it that the reformers decided "not to answer defiance with defiance, but to have moderate conduct shame arrogant violence." It was the nuanced sophistication of their response that made possible today's complex society.

Now, many people here tonight could rise to point out examples of violence in our history or a lack of ethical behaviour or of non-respect for minorities. And I would agree. Have there been failures? Yes. Great injustices ignored? Absolutely. Betrayals? Unfortunately, yes. Hypocrisy? Waves of it. After all, what I am describing is a real society, not a nationalistic publicity stunt. And the point of memory is also to remember the failures. And to judge these against the main trajectory of society. Each time we do not respond with "moderate conduct" to justified or unjustified provocation, we inflict a new suppurating wound on ourselves, and it alters our memory. Most societies are destroyed by the accumulated weight of their self-inflicted wounds. It could be argued that by the standards of Western civilization our wounds are infrequent and small. Still, they are there. They are real. And they never disappear.

However, the obvious point about the reformers is that they succeeded. The burning of the Parliament buildings was one of our greatest successes — or, rather, the way it was handled was a great success. And the Lord Durham school of doom and gloom about what these minorities would do to each other turned out, quite simply, to be wrong.

What's more, once you have focused on the remarkable success story of the late 1840s and early '50s, you can't help rethinking the almost religious status conferred upon a few of our Fathers of Confederation. They are habitually presented to us as the creators of a country out of dust in 1867, propelled forward only by the impatient leadership of the imperial government and by their own imaginations and ambitions. In truth, they operated with their imaginations dominated not by London or Paris or the neighbours to the south, or, indeed, by the failures of Mackenzie and Papineau, but by the successful model that LaFontaine and Baldwin and Howe had created twenty years before. The concern of the Fathers of Confederation — both those who supported Confederation and those who opposed it, including Howe — was that they would fail to live up to that model. Some did. Some didn't. What was the model? Let me summarize it in this way: after 133 years of this unusual experiment, we have killed in political strife among ourselves less than a hundred citizens — most of them on a single day at Batoche.

Even one is, of course, one too many. But compared with any other Western democracy, the number is almost miraculous. You may consider this an odd reflection, but I think the first measure of any citizen-based culture must be not its rhetoric or myths or leaders or laws but how few of its own citizens it kills.

Nineteenth-century statesmen read a good deal of Greek literature. When exactly, how exactly, did LaFontaine and Baldwin find the right way to respond that night, as Montreal exploded? I like to think that one of them had been reading Euripides — *The Bacchae* — and had noted the solid advice of Teresias:

[P]ay heed to my words. You rely
On force; but it is not force that governs human affairs.
Do not mistake for wisdom that opinion which
May rise from a sick mind....
[I]n all matters, self-control
Resides in our own natures.

At this point you might think that I've taken us quite a way away from those four to five thousand people who are close around us in this city tonight and yet are without homes. Not at all. I've been talking about the foundations of your society and mine, foundations built upon a conscious intellectual concept of, and therefore dependent upon, ethics and principle. These principles assume moderation, inclusion and citizen-based legitimacy.

I therefore feel comfortable saying that on the basis of such a foundation, it is not possible to imagine that such a state of poverty — of exclusion — as four to five thousand homeless a night in one city is normal or part of the way things have to be.

To which someone might reply that things have changed, conditions have changed, technology, global markets, inter-dependency. We can no longer be held responsible for our past engagements? I won't go on. You know the line. In reply I could, without trying to avoid our failures, nevertheless trace the LaFontaine-Baldwin trajectory event by event, over the past 152 years.

There is the prairie farmer reform movement of the early twentieth century that took up the inclusive ideal of the early reformers and redefined it for the twentieth century, for all of Canada, introducing everything from votes for women to transfer payments to medicare. I could even argue that le modèle québécois is in large part the result of the prairie farmers' model — and that is a compliment to both parties.

And out of that prairie movement I could trace the evolution of Clifford Sifton, the great newspaper baron, capitalist and politician who organized the settlement of the west under Laurier. You would hear him speaking out in the late 1920s about our drift away from this society's real trajectory; about "frenzied finance … the purpose of which is to inflate the capital of corporations serving the public, and to load onto the public the subsequent necessity of paying dividends on inflated capital." Along the way he clarified the role of the press: "It is no part of a newspaper's function to defend a corporation; a corporation is always well able to defend itself."

And out of that I could trace the career of the greatest philosopher and economist Canada has yet produced — Harold Innis, of Robert Baldwin's university — saying, in a multitude of ways, "[M]aterialism is the auxiliary doctrine of every tyranny."

And parallel to that, the remarkable Monseigneur Charbonneau, Archevêque de Montréal, standing up in his cathedral on May 1, 1949, during the Asbestos strike and preaching before a hostile premier and establishment that "nous nous attachons plus à l'homme qu'au capital.... [Q]ue l'on cesse d'accorder plus d'attention aux intérêts d'argent qu'à l'élément humain."

Of course, that is still fifty years ago, and the counter-argument would still be that since then things have changed. Things have changed is the standard answer to any suggestion that memory is important.

Let me deal, therefore, with this idea that something called progress or change can wipe out something called memory or the trajectory of a society. The underlying idea seems to be that for the first time in twenty-five hundred years of Western civilization things have changed so drastically that the public good must automatically give way before technology and self-interest. This argument reminds me of what Robert Baldwin called the struggle of "the might of public opinion against fashion and corruption."

Of course things have changed. They have always changed. Sometimes more, sometimes less. But nothing has happened over the past quarter century that has had an unredeemable, inevitable, searing effect on our link to our past. On our ability to enforce our ethical standards. Or on the power of citizens to engage in responsible individualism. It is an insult to our intelligence and to the redeeming value of positive change to suggest that we are its passive victim, that it *must* dehumanize us and separate us from the reality of our ethics.

Let me give you three examples of the deforming nature that change can have when it is treated as a great avenging god. The phenomenon that I call corporatism has affected the ability of every sector of society to act. Indeed, we have all become used to acting out our specialist dramas within our specialist relationships. In that way, whether in Europe or Australia or North America, society has truly been divided into interest groups — some of them against the public good, some indifferent, some in favour, but all acting outside of the inclusive mechanisms of democracy.

Think of areas such as social work or environmentalism. These subjects fill the airwaves, fill the newspapers. We have the impression that we have learned a great deal about the problems these movements deal with — from the homeless to pollution. In Sydney, in Paris, here, in Berlin, we sense a certain agreement for action within the society. And yet that action, when it does come, rarely matches the strength of the movement or the public support for it. But, and this is my point, if we turn to our elected assemblies — at all levels and indeed in almost all countries — we discover that there are very few elected social workers or environmentalists.

In the late nineteenth century, parliaments, such as the French Assembly, the Canadian House of Commons, the American House of Representatives, were filled with lawyers, because we were busy putting in place the necessary legal infrastructures. Today, in most assemblies, lawyers represent only some 15 percent of the elected representatives; managers of various sorts have increased to 15 percent; business people another 15 percent. But, for example, in Ottawa, only two MPs identify themselves as environmentalists. And I'm sure that they won't mind my pointing out that they belong to the first wave of environmentalists. The younger generations are not in the democratic process. They are caught up in their parallel work in NGOs [non-governmental organizations], as are the social workers.

Now, NGO work is fascinating. It is good work. But the structures being used are corporatist. And we live, throughout the West, in democracies — that is, in places in which changes are made through the democratic process. In a curious way, the very success of those NGOs most devoted to the public good actually undermines the democratic process — the real guarantor of the public good — because they don't feed into it.

I'm not suggesting that elected houses be reduced to collections of interest groups. I'm saying that reform tends to come when the reformers integrate themselves into the democratic process. If they stay outside, they reduce themselves to lobbyists — and a lobbyist is a lobbyist is a lobbyist, whether the cause is good or bad. The problem is that the courtier-like features required to be an effective lobbyist are usually better suited to causes that undermine the public good than to those that support it.

So long as a good cause is outside the political process, it will be subject to the argument that there isn't the money, or there are other priorities or, inevitably, that things have changed. Let me put this argument a different way. So long as an NGO — which could also be defined as a corporation of social reformers — remains outside the democratic system, it has no real political levers. Its activists are not there, in the people's chamber, to clarify the cause. And there is no practical link between the problem they are devoted to and the real action required to deal with it. PR victories — which NGOs so often win — cannot be converted automatically into law. Nor should they be. Again, we live in democracies. But the result is that there are no direct practical links between the public debate and government action. The public therefore becomes discouraged about the effectiveness of politics, because politics appear to be unresponsive to the public debate. And because of their disconnection from the formal political process, the corporations of social reformers themselves begin to look naïve. All of this results in what playwright René-Daniel Dubois calls "la perte d'une culture partagée" — a fractured culture or a fractured society.

Before you know it, poverty has been intellectually reconfigured into a condition of society — an inevitability — while at a human level it is treated as a personal failure. Suddenly society seems unable to respond with nuanced sophistication to what actually is natural and inevitable about human beings — that is, differences in personality, in ambition, in mental aptitude, in opportunities.

In other words, so long as a good cause remains on the outside, it may actually give comfort to those who oppose it. A cause really only makes ethical, utilitarian and social sense when it and its proponents are integrated into the democratic process. I'm not suggesting the NGOs have no valid role. Involvement in democratic politics does not mean that any individual must abandon parallel reform movements. We are all capable of doing two things at once, of being two people.

The current withdrawal of most social reformers from our democratic process is certainly a change in our society, but I don't think it was inevitable or is eternal. It is merely a side effect of corporatism. Once we realize that, and realize that both democracy and the causes of reform are suffering, well, a realignment will begin.

A second example: fashion throughout the West has it that we must move away from overarching, all-inclusive public programs in favour of targeted programs. But the targeting of need — which is what it comes down to — takes us back to the old top-down, judgmental and eventually moralizing approach towards those citizens who have problems. In fact, this is false efficiency because it removes the simplicity of inclusion and replaces it with an outdated, highly charged, labour-intensive managerial approach.

I'm not suggesting that our current systems don't have problems. But these have nothing to do with "universality" or ethical inclusiveness. They have to do with the weakness of rational linear management.

The point of targeted programs is that they not only bring back judgmental administration, they bring back plain old charity. This is now presented as citizens taking on more responsibility for others. But if they can afford that responsibility, they can afford the taxes that would ensure we do not slip into a society of noblesse oblige in which those *with* get to choose who and how to help those *without*.

As Strindberg put it in his blunt and accurate way, "All charity is humiliating." Perhaps it isn't surprising that charity was one of the weapons used by the opponents of Canadian democracy in the 1840s. Sir Charles Metcalfe, the autocratic governor general, was famous for his largesse as he attempted to buy support. He was lauded by the anti-democratic elites as "a fortune spender in public charity."

Ethics is quite different. It doesn't require the gratitude of the recipient, i.e., the humiliation of the recipient. The ego of the donor is not stroked. There is no warm, self-indulgent feeling of having done good. Ethics is a much cooler business than charity. That is why the concept of arm's length goes with that of the public good. Ethics is about citizens being treated equally. And in that sense, it is all important that we concentrate on the difference between the role of the citizen and that of the state. The citizen owns the state and receives from it neither charity nor the generosity of noblesse oblige. What the citizen receives is meant to be, as Baldwin put it, appropriate to "the happy conduct of public affairs."

I'm not suggesting for a moment that there is no room for charity. Or that the line between charity and obligation is ever clear. But charity cannot replace, in an inclusive democracy, the organization of the public good. And if it does, well, then it excludes citizens from their role as citizens because they are dependent on another. Citizenship is about obligation, not about choosing to be generous.

But then *things have changed.* We are told that because of globalization we can no longer count on the obligation of the citizen. For example, apparently we can no longer count on nation-states being able to raise taxes in a competitive world economy. And so increasingly we must hope that generous individuals will give as best they can. In fact, our ability to apply the idea of obligation to citizenship is fatally weakened because, we are told, the nation-state as we have known it is finished. Has been severely weakened. Is probably on its way out.

It is very curious. I have noticed that the people who talk most triumphantly of the victory of democracy over various ideologies are the same people who talk about the nation-state being dead, powerless, or words to that effect. They often manage their triumphalism and their dirge in the same paragraph.

But the thing is this. Democracy was and is entirely constructed inside the structure of the Western nation-state. Democracy is an emanation of the nation-state. And now that most of the unpleasant nationalist, racial, imperial characteristics of our nations have been eliminated, democracy, citizenship, obligation and the public good remain as their greatest glory.

The other curious thing is that those who announce the death of the nation-state usually do so with a little self-satisfied smile.

Well, if the nation-state is dead, so is democracy. Then it is not the state that has passed away, but the power of the citizen. And passed away in favour of what? Of the transnational? Nobody could take such an argument seriously unless their income depended in some way on believing that the nation-state was finished.

I don't think that this chronicle of a death foretold is accurate. And not because I believe in the force or virtues of nationalism. Rather, I believe in the aggressive intelligence of the citizenry, as against the ultimately self-destructive nature of corporatism and the passive, inefficient, top-heavy directionlessness of the trans-national. Individuals have not struggled centuries to establish an idea of responsibility and a sense of the concrete, inclusive public good in order to give it all away simply because some transient technology and heavy-handed interest groups have been declared by mysterious, unknown forces to be in charge.

In any case, what is presented today as a great monolithic absolute truth called Globalization is merely one particular, indeed narrow, version of internationalism. There are dozens of other possible versions. There is nothing brilliant or inevitable

about this particular model. If anything, it resembles an unso-
phisticated version of late-nineteenth-century dogma.

Frankly, it doesn't even meet its own standards. It is declared
to be a victory for the marketplace, yet it is rushing towards
monopolies and oligopolies in sector after sector. Anyone who is
in favour of capitalism and competition must be against these
old monopolistic forms. We know that, among other things,
private-sector monopolies make up for their ineffectiveness by
limiting progress in order to create an illusion of stability.

In any case, we can already see the nation-states reacting. On
the negative side, there is the return of false populism. Austria is
just the latest example, and this phenomenon is in part a protest
against the citizen's sense of powerlessness.

On the positive side, a great deal more is happening. There
are early but widespread moves underway to regulate the international money markets. Australia has balked at engaging in a
number of the recent economic fashions. New Zealand, the fairy
tale of the economic determinists, is reversing directions. One
senses the leadership of the G7 growing nervous over the power
of the unregulated transnationals. Even the OECD is calling for
controls. I'm not suggesting that we are headed back to 1960.
Or that we should be. I am saying that the force at the core of
our trajectory — and that of many other countries — is the citizenry. And they have been presented with an unrealistic picture
in which economics has been internationalized through dozens
of complex binding treaties, while democracy, social policy, most
of justice, work conditions and taxation powers have been left,
hobbled, at the national level.

The citizens will either require changes to the international
economic arrangements that will permit, for example, sufficient
levels of national taxation and regulation. Or they will require

international agreements in all of those other areas. Or some combination of the two.

Too late, some will say. No turning back now. Things have changed. Globalization is inevitable.

Well, for better and for worse, nothing is inevitable. Only ideologues believe in determinism. And economic fashions usually last no more than twenty-five years. Besides, the moment something is declared to be inevitable, you know you are approaching a major swing around, often in the opposite direction.

And now, let me offer a third and final portrait of fashion pretending to be revolutionary change. It goes like this. The world is one small place, therefore everything in it must be big. Big companies and big government departments. Everything must be merged to meet the challenge of global smallness. The logic is hazy. The theory, however, is that these continual mergers and the rapid emergence of monopolies and oligopolies is a logical outcome of the international marketplace. This is nonsense from a business point of view. The best way to progress, function, make profits in such a large single market is to be small or medium-sized — that is, to be fast and flexible. The worst is to be a slow, directionless technocratic haven. Even as these mergers go crashing on — and failing at a rate of about 80 percent — you can sense a more intelligent undercurrent in the marketplace going in the opposite direction.

The truth is that gigantism — which is what we are now experiencing — is a managerial ideal. It has nothing to do with the market. It has to do with the standard, late-nineteenth-century, technocratic technique in which power equals control and more power equals a need for control over a larger structure. Gigantism is pure form over content, to say nothing of personal self-indulgence for a few individuals. It is also a fashion that will probably last less than a decade.

In any case, it is expansion in the absence of ideas. A few months ago in Australia I came across a vibrant advertisement on the hoarding around a large expansion building site for a department store chain.

DAVID JONES
Bringing you an exciting
Shopping experience
for the
New Millennium

If you haven't got anything else to do for the next thousand years, why not?

The point is that very large corporations do not work as effective players in a competitive marketplace. They are slow, inefficient and seek monopoly or oligopoly status. Very large government departments do a bit better, as their purpose is the administration of vast non-competitive services. But they have difficulty giving direction. And public policy works only when it is driven by ideas. When it is driven by form and management, it collapses.

I'd like to close tonight with the possibility of a real change — one that relates to the trajectory of our society. It is as relevant to our past as to our future — both to the citizen's role, whether homeless or comfortable, and to making sense of globalization.

The brief description I gave a little while ago of LaFontaine and Baldwin's three-year government was that of a massive consolidation of the ideas that had been in the air for years. I spoke after that of the key role lawyers played in our nineteenth-century parliaments. They were organizing a society in desperate need of legal shape. But already, in his resignation speech in September 1851, Louis LaFontaine was talking about the need for law reform.

Le danger aujourd'hui, c'est la facilité avec laquelle on fait des lois. Si l'on continue, notre code sera bientôt un labyrinthe dans lequel personne ne pourra se retrouver.

Joseph Howe was a little funnier on the same subject:

Every law could be reduced to half its size and made twice as effective. A reward should be offered for the best and smallest act on any subject.

I'll give you a contemporary example of this. As a writer, I really ought to understand the libel laws. I don't. Neither do most lawyers. But how can you have effective freedom of speech if nobody can understand its legal limits?

What I am talking about is much more than law reform. For half a century we have been busy putting in place, on an ad hoc basis, structures and programs that have successfully produced a reasonably just society, at least in comparison with what came before. This ad hoc method is normal in a democracy. Each small advance is the result of debate and then of legislation.

Our accomplishments, however, now resemble a large mound filled with legal and administrative details. For most people, whether citizens on the outside or working on the inside, it is an impenetrable mass. There is never a view of the whole, or even of an entire single logic within the whole.

The more complex this has become, the more it has encouraged the worst in our managerial societies. By that I mean a
narrow corporatist approach — a world of consultants and of
specialist dialects, of stakeholders and of confused, frustrated
citizens. And more and more ad hoc changes.

Not surprisingly, as the mound builds up, the managerial
solutions tend to deal increasingly with narrow issues, one at a
time, and in the short term. That is one of the explanations for
why we have regressed into need-based programs.

What I am describing is a curiosity of democratic societies.
We start out with a long view and a desire to create inclusive
programs. Democracy, rightfully, requires that we create them in
an ad hoc manner. Over the short term this is fine. But if we
leave them in an ad hoc form, they gradually become the opposite of what we originally intended.

Perhaps the most important job to be done over the past
twenty years was to take this enormous ad hoc mound of law
and regulation and administrative detail and to consolidate it —
to clarify, boil down, rediscover the shape of it. This was not
done. The result would have been, could still be, to reunite the
citizens with their state.

At first a project like this doesn't sound too exciting. But the
obscurity of the mound is one of the key elements preventing
citizens from participating as citizens. And consolidation is
always the essential second step to be taken after an initial
chaotic rush to reform. Most of the programs we have put in
place in the democratic manner still work surprisingly well,
especially considering their structure. But those who believe in
the original reforms have made the mistake over the past few
years of defending the ad hoc jumble of their form rather than
the underlying principles. As a result, most reforms undertaken

over the past twenty years in the name of efficiency have actually resulted in less delivery of programs and more cost. Why? Because they are an attempt to micromanage large, complex subjects.

These contemporary false reformers should have been in the forefront of the battle for consolidation, flying the flag of ideas, intent and ethics. Instead they have defended structure and so have found themselves marginalized by those who do not believe and who use the now unnecessary complexity of the mound as an excuse to undo the actual accomplishments of the reforms.

There was a desperate need twenty years ago — a need that is now even more desperate — to take that leap into consolidation. If such a consolidation were to be successful, it would prepare the way for a whole new wave of creative reforms. And I believe that those reforms would take the shape of clear, overarching and determinedly inclusive policies. Fewer, but all-inclusive, programs would be far cheaper and far more effective.

I'm not suggesting for a moment that four to five thousand homeless people in Toronto will have to wait for those changes in order to see their situation improve. But I am certain that we would see this whole problem quite differently if we saw it in the light of clear, simple, inclusive policies. One of the hardest things to do in public policy is to marry ethics with effective programs. The cool arm's-length approach of ethics combined with simple, clear, all-inclusive policies can make that happen. And that would be an honest reflection of the trajectory that Louis LaFontaine and Robert Baldwin sent our way.

Alain Dubuc

〜 2ND ANNUAL LAFONTAINE-BALDWIN LECTURE

École des Hautes Études Commerciales de Montréal
Montreal, Quebec
Friday, March 9, 2001

Traduction du texte prononcé aux HEC

One year ago, I wrote a series of editorials in *La Presse* on the political blind alley that Quebec finds itself in, deadlocked between two political projects: the sovereigntist movement, lacking enough supporters to set in motion a process that would lead to separation; and the reform of federalism, with insufficient numbers of Canadians willing to sponsor the dreamed-of constitutional changes.

My theory was that in order to escape the stalemate, the province would have to change paradigms, to define collective goals that fit more closely with the needs of contemporary Quebec. But the primary obstacle to this redeployment of priorities is the weight of a nationalism that has not evolved in tune with society and that, with its dogmas, its myths, its sacred cows, its empty symbols, has become a barrier to Quebec's development.

I mention those articles because they have something to do with my being here this evening, and because they no doubt gave John Saul and the Dominion Institute the idea of entrusting me with the considerable responsibility of delivering the second LaFontaine-Baldwin lecture.

As I prepared this address, my first inclination was to elaborate on certain elements from my series of editorials. But, after careful consideration, I changed my mind.

First, because it would have been too easy: I'm sure that a critique of Quebec nationalism would be a hit with an English-Canadian audience. But this type of success wouldn't get us very far. And it would in no way mirror the spirit of my editorials, which were not meant to seduce my readers, but to force a debate on a very sensitive and very controversial subject in Quebec.

And also because it becomes tiresome, in cross-Canada forums, to be the Quebecer who presents a Quebec point of view. It's a reflection, I feel, of the sort of isolation in which Quebecers of every stripe have shut themselves up, with the result that they have taken so little interest and involved themselves so negligibly in Canadian debates that they have ceased to be relevant.

For those reasons I've chosen to speak to you not of Quebec, but of Canada. And to use my series not as a way of tackling the Quebec question, but as an analytical grid that could be used to ponder Canadian reality.

This exercise leads me to believe that the nationalisms of Canada and Quebec are close cousins, or even Siamese twins, and, despite important differences, the similarities are dramatic. Canada suffers in many respects from the same ailments as Quebec. In fact, Canadian nationalism is also in the process of congealing under the weight of myths and dogmas that are becoming obstacles to the country's evolution.

The Ills of Quebec Nationalism

I know that Quebec nationalism worries and annoys English Canada: through its militant aspects, its flags, because of the conflicts that have brought us into opposition — but also because people often tend to confuse the nationalist sentiment shared by most French-speaking Quebecers with the sovereigntist current and with the passionate outpourings and ethnocentrism of the more inflamed militants. But there are more sober ways of defining it. And one is the sense, shared by a solid majority of Quebecers, of having a distinct identity, of constituting a nation, and of wishing that this nation be recognized and have the means to fulfill itself. On these points there is great consensus in Quebec.

This sense will not disappear, and must not disappear, because it rests on a verifiable sociological reality: the existence of a people, with its dominant language, its culture, its history and institutions and its difficult relationships with the majority that demand special considerations.

The sense of constituting a nation and the will to build on it can be an extremely rich source of energy, a factor of social cohesiveness that leads to progress. But again, it is necessary that this national sense be in touch with the evolution of society. If it is static, it can be a terrible check on social progress, and if it is exalted, it can easily become a tool of exclusion rather than a window on the world. Which leads me to emphasize the necessity of distinguishing between a nationalism that is productive and modern and a nationalism that is backward-looking.

While writing my editorials, I'd thought to use the concept of good and bad nationalism and to draw a parallel, which I hoped would be humorous, with cholesterol. But friends pointed out that the world of lipids, infinitely more complex than you can imagine, does not divide cholesterols simply into the good and the bad (the example of omega-3 fatty acids will do). And when you consider the subject for any length of time, nationalism becomes a lot more complex as well.

I do not believe that present-day Quebec nationalism is reactionary. But we don't have to scratch very deep to bring those angry reflexes to life, above all in times of crisis and tension. For that force to travel in the right direction, it must be monitored, be made the subject of debate, and it must also be managed.

What struck me in the case of Quebec was that the excesses of our nationalism seemed to be explainable by the weight of history. It is normal that Quebec's national sense find its roots in the past, since the Quebec difference and the Canadian duality are the product of three centuries of history. But what is less normal is the interpretation of the history that has nourished the Quebec myth.

Our nationalism, for a long time a survival tool, was largely inspired by the numerous defeats that marked the tribulations of the French in America over the centuries, from the Plains of Abraham to Meech Lake. Its heroes are often losers: Montcalm, Dollard des Ormeaux, de Lorimier, Riel, the Patriotes, or even René Lévesque, who founded the Parti Québécois but lost his referendum.

A people must not forget where they come from. But it's not because we should be inspired by our history that we must necessarily revel in the past. This nationalism fed by history in effect created an image of ourselves that does not correspond to reality. It has perpetuated the pain of oppression long after the oppression itself disappeared. It has shaped a culture of losers, something that Quebecers have not been for quite some time. The relative oppression that French speakers have been subject to, the economic injustices they've been the victims of, a certain exclusion from the circles of power, the sense of inferiority — these have disappeared; but the memory remains, vivid enough to affect behaviours.

Wrote Paul Valéry: "History is the most dangerous product that the chemistry of the intellect ever evolved. Its properties are well known. It makes us dream, it intoxicates people, creates false memories for them, exaggerates their reactions, keeps their old wounds open, torments their rest, leads them to delusions of grandeur or of persecution, and makes nations bitter, arrogant, insufferable and vain." I have to confess that I've taken this passage to heart.

This is what we have to get rid of when breaking the chains of the past. Because the weight of history and the defeatist culture to which it gave rise continue to affect our behaviour, continue to determine our socio-political agenda, continue to colour our strategies.

For instance, remember the "humiliation" period of Lucien Bouchard, happily over. Or the contemptible "l'argent et des votes ethniques" (money and ethnic votes) that Jacques Parizeau, a man of sophistication notwithstanding, delivered himself of in a moment of despair, which had less to do with xenophobia than with the paranoia of minorities. Or again the language issue, potentially the most emotional and explosive component of the national debate, where that same attitude of the eternal loser seems to be at work.

It is also the case with Quebec's great battles. For a half century, succeeding governments in Quebec City have fought to protect provincial jurisdictions and expand their area of authority. Along with recognition of its distinct character, this has constituted one of the two major axes in Quebec's struggle to redefine its place within the federal regime.

But the way in which Quebec conducts this legitimate struggle also reflects the weight of the years.

Because of the battle that's been raging for two generations, the so-called traditional demands of Quebec are moving further and further away from the true needs of Quebecers. The matter of the sharing of powers is indeed an important one, but it still does not justify the extent of emotion reserved for it, or, more precisely, it does so no longer.

But Quebec political tradition does not allow for putting things in perspective, for taking minor conflicts with a grain of salt, for distinguishing between a battle royal and a skirmish. Over five decades, Quebec has forged dogmas that no politician can ignore without fear of excommunication.

The weight of the years imposes a tradition, which is expressed in a martial vocabulary, full of superlatives — victories, retreats, penetrations, even extreme combat — that reinforce the sense of urgency and seriousness. It is a choke-hold that forces our leaders to choose the path of war, not because of the importance of the stakes, but because old battles are involved in which it is no longer possible to retreat.

Nationalism also finds expression in the pride we take in certain of its realizations. This is certainly progress. But pride, when expressed in a rigid context, can have perverse effects. Such is the case with the achievements of the Quiet Revolution, consecrated, defined as an integral part of the Quebec identity, and therefore untouchable. Pride, interpreted this way, instead of inspiring vitality and movement becomes, on the contrary, a justification for failure to act.

The result: Quebec is imprisoned in a political debate without issue between an undesired sovereignty and an impossible reform of federalism. This much we know. But that political impasse has given rise to other constraints. Those of a province that is more indebted, more taxed than the others and that offers fewer services. Those of a province that is poorer, but incapable of acquiring the tools that would secure it greater growth.

A Nationalism Unaware of Itself

Et voilà pour le nationalisme québécois. But can we find, in this Quebec experience, useful lessons for Canadian nationalism?

First, we have to ask ourselves whether Canadian nationalism really exists. The answer should be obvious, but it seems that many Canadians tend to negate its presence and are often unaware that certain of their attitudes, their gestures or their debates are expressions of such a nationalism.

Yes, Canadian nationalism exists. It rests on an obvious identity, rooted in an attachment to a territory Canadians have pioneered and whose integrity they do not wish to see threatened by a secession. It rests on a history, on political and social values, on a culture, on the coexistence of two official languages, on traditions, on lifestyles, on a vision of the role the country plays in the world, on institutions.

This sense of a nation runs through the entire spectrum of expressions: from the elite nationalism shaped by Pierre Trudeau's vision to the grassroots nationalism of Preston Manning, from the pride in the role played by Canada on the international stage to the wonderful "My name is Joe and I am Canadian." This cri de cœur, spontaneous and unsubsidized, has done more for the Canadian psyche than all of Sheila Copps's flags.

But Canadians are often unaware of the manifestations of their own nationalism. How many times has the constitutional crisis been presented as the result of pressures arising from Quebec nationalism — that eternal troublemaker — rather than as a confrontation of two nationalisms, whose visions are different and sometimes incompatible?

When we examine the conflicts that have brought Quebec and Canada into opposition, and in particular the last conflict, Meech Lake, it becomes plain that the seriousness of the crisis can be explained only by the fact that the Quebec demands, in a remarkable mirror effect, met up with an obstinacy every bit as symbolic and every bit as irrational on the other side.

Meech was the confrontation of identity myths in their purest form, where Quebec turned its demands into a life-or-death issue, but where Canada was ready to be torn apart, ready to risk breaking up rather than recognize a difference that would call into question its own vision of the country, including the completely absurd cult of the strict equality of the ten provinces.

The denial of Canadian nationalism can be found as well in those attempts to grade nationalisms — to define some variants as more noble than others, to oppose Canada's civic nationalism to Quebec's ethnic one. The question is not to determine who has the better nationalism — a childish sort of exercise — but to note that whenever it ennobles its own nationalism, a society will have a tendency to turn a blind eye to the more undesirable manifestations of it, and to disengage itself from its obligations to be vigilant.

The reality is more complex. Canada's nationalisms are hybrid phenomena. The Canadian variety has its origins in an ethnic nationalism, essentially British, which to be sure has undergone alterations with the intermixing of populations but which, over the decades, has experienced spasms of exclusion. Quebec nationalism, on the other hand, much more ethnic when it reflected the struggle of French Canadians, has for a long time rested less on ethnic origins than on language and culture, and, to the degree that the population of Quebec is undergoing a transformation, it is itself evolving in the direction of a civic nationalism.

Their dynamics are clearly different and reflect different social realities, among them the fact that Quebec nationalism is that of a minority, one that rightly or wrongly feels itself under threat and so must exhibit a constant degree of tension in the face of the majority — but one that entertains no doubt as to its identity. Canadian nationalism does not undergo that constant pressure; however, it must take greater care in defining the parameters of an identity whose borders are less focused and more fragile, and that sometimes rests on a certain voluntarism.

Where the two come together in a remarkable way is that both of them are built on a culture of dominated peoples, Quebecers being losers and Canadians being underdogs. French speakers feel dominated by English Canada, and to a lesser extent by English-speaking North America. Canada, dominated by a British Empire from which it belatedly broke free, lives in constant fear of American domination, and in moments of crisis is quick to mobilize in the face of threats from French Quebec. In both cases, we're dealing with reactive nationalism, triggered by threats, real or imagined, insecurity and fears: fear of free trade, fear of Quebec, fear of English-language pressures, fear of disappearing. And fear, as we know, is a collective sentiment that rarely brings a people to progress.

These obvious similarities are in large measure explained by the fact that the two nations share centuries of interaction, and, though lacking a common history, they have a common past, as well as the common values of the country they've built.

And there are instances where the two nationalisms, antagonistic though they may be, evoke exactly the same symbols to establish identities they judge to be different: the social-security safety net, for example, which is essentially the same, and which Quebecers as much as Canadians perceive as an integral element of their own identity.

But where Canadian nationalism differs markedly is in the fact that it has no guidelines. And the consequence of Canadians tending to be ignorant of the existence of their own nationalism, or not seeing its manifestations, is potentially costly. Nationalism, here as everywhere, has its dangers; it can lead to excess and loss of control. For nationalism to be a positive force, it needs managing.

In this respect, the situation is more worrying in Canada than in Quebec, because Canada has no fail-safe mechanism.

Quebec is obviously not perfect: the national question has generated its share of excesses. But we have mechanisms to limit loss of control, because we've lived so long with this national debate that we're acutely aware of its dangers. And also because we are politically divided, which provides us with watchdogs: federalist Quebecers who keep a close eye on sovereigntist excesses; English Canadians, always extremely vigilant where Quebec is concerned; and even the self-discipline of principled or image-conscious sovereigntists. Thus, when Jacques Parizeau, on the evening of his referendum defeat, spoke of "l'argent et les votes ethniques," he survived in office for twenty-four hours.

These checks and balances do not exist in Canada, because English Canadians are not aware enough of their own nationalism and because they are not divided on the unity issue: everyone is federalist, almost everyone reacts badly to the prospect of Quebec's separation, everyone shares a love of the country. (A revealing semantic detail should be noticed. What in Quebec we call the national debate or the Canada–Quebec debate or the constitutional debate has been defined in English Canada as the Unity debate, a term that contains its own values from the get-go and provides a fine example of Newspeak, so that anyone not sharing the Canadian point of view stands, by definition, against unity.)

The result is that no mechanisms exist to control nationalist excess. Some examples?

In my arena, that of print journalism, because of the divisions within my readership it is impossible to present extreme positions. There is such an imposed self-discipline that there are no Quebec equivalents of Diane Francis. There's no one in Quebec in upper management at a respectable publication read by a sophisticated public, for example, vicious enough to call for the imprisonment of elected politicians.

But the most revealing example of the loss of control of Canadians over their nationalism is probably the partitionist movement that arose in western Quebec in the days that followed the referendum almost won by the sovereigntists, in which anglophone municipalities sought to remain within

Canada in the event of Quebec's secession. The movement, fraught with emotion, was understandable at the human level and reflected the trauma of people whose lives had almost been turned upside down.

The experience of the past decade, which has given rise to the formation of many new states, has taught us that the partitionist model, wherein portions of a new state remain attached to the previous state, has been applied in only one country, the former Yugoslavia. And that paved the way for a monstrous dynamic. Canada is, of course, not Serbia. But it is clear that the temptation of partition, in the event of a Yes victory, would lead Canada to choose the most explosive model of secession management imaginable.

And yet, that model, which should have been condemned out of hand because of the spiral of violence it risks producing, incompatible with Canadian traditions, was actually encouraged by the Chrétien government. And why? Because that partitionist movement was useful at the political level, in that its underlying thesis, the non-integrity of Quebec territory, could be used as a means of undercutting the sovereigntist cause.

This, in my view, is the typical case of a nationalist deviation whereby a nation, feeling itself threatened, develops defence mechanisms that fall outside the bounds of acceptable behaviour.

The Ills of Canadian Nationalism

The purpose of these remarks is not to launch myself on an attack of Canadian nationalism, but rather to underscore the idea that Canadians must take great pains to reflect on their identity, to define it, to trace precisely the outline of their nationalism; that herein lies the subject of a necessary debate. This is all the more necessary in that Canadian nationalism, like its counterpart in Quebec, is founded on a certain number of myths.

Canadians, often unsure of themselves, have erected a monument that would both better define Canada and enhance their self-esteem. This was a noble and healthy process; it lay at the basis of the vision of a modern Canada so fully embodied in the person of Pierre Trudeau.

Of course, there are characteristics of the Canadian identity that are deeply rooted: a history relatively free of violence, for instance; a capacity for coexistence among different cultures. But the fact remains that the three elements that probably most accurately define the Canadian identity are not the products of spontaneous generation. They are the products of human intervention and are extremely recent creations. I refer here to the attachment to a form of justice concerned with rights that finds special expression in the Charter of Rights and Freedoms. To a respect for plurality and difference, including multiculturalism. And to the values of generosity and sharing that underlie the social-security safety net.

The Charter, so essential to Canadian identity, is less than twenty years old; the very idea of multiculturalism is thirty years old; the welfare state began to take shape fifty years ago.

We could, at first glance, see in all this a sign of modernity, the ability of a society to define new values. But what fascinates is the speed with which these new values became sacred cows, which, in my view, is a reflection of an insecurity so great that Canadians have been led to seek life preservers rather than development tools.

We find the same thing in Quebec, where here as well the sacred cows are remarkably young — should we be talking of sacred calves? The Révolution tranquille — the Quiet Revolution — is forty years old; Bill 101 is twenty-five; and "le modèle québécois" is no more than about thirty.

The most striking phenomenon is that of the Charter. However much the principles of justice that it embodies derive from Canadian values, the tool — a charter in the American style and foreign to our legal traditions — is itself very recent. But this document, whose implications we have not yet digested, has already been internalized as a central element in the Canadian identity, to the point that it is no longer possible to deviate from it. In this adoption, as sudden as it has been absolute, there is something suspect that leads us to wonder how it was possible to be Canadian a quarter century ago.

Even if Canada has always had a tradition of immigration, the idea of pluralism that Canada holds to was essentially reformulated when multiculturalism became a cardinal virtue some thirty years ago, partly in response to the two-nations thesis and to the rising sovereigntist tide.

We are, I believe, in the presence of a myth here. It is true that Canada is a land of diversity, a land where tolerance has successfully taken root. But when we look at Canada's recent history, and even harder at its older history, we quite quickly discover that Canadian society stands up rather badly to the shock of difference. Canada deals well with a mosaic society, especially because the great diversity of the sources of immigration has a way of minimizing any threat. But Canada reacts quite badly when that diversity oversteps the boundaries of folklore and threatens the dominant culture.

We've seen, in the case of Quebec, how difficult it is for English Canada to accept the principle that part of the population can be different, and to formally recognize it — something that constitutes the very essence of respect for diversity. We've seen it with the First Nations, with whom we're still painfully seeking a way of coexisting in difference. We're seeing it now with the populations of the western provinces, who try to assert themselves through values that diverge from dogmas established in central Canada.

The perception — a false one, in our view — that Canada has of its own tolerance is accompanied by another perception, equally erroneous, about the behaviours that accompany this openness. And it's the image of gentleness that has led Canada to think it can resolve its internal crises through love — what we might call a touchy-feely nationalism.

This was the approach that gave us the love-in in Montreal on October 27, 1995, a few days before the referendum, when Canadians came to tell Quebecers how much they loved them.

This was an event that left me deeply uncomfortable, first of all, for conceptual reasons. The general theme of love strikes me as an approach that, in terms of resolving conflicts among peoples, is naïve and inappropriate. It's true that Canadians of all origins, unlike what we tend to find in other binational or multinational states, carry on cordial relationships at the individual level. Montreal has never been Belfast.

It's rare for nations or communities that coexist in a single country to love one another. On the contrary, the very existence of multinational societies is usually the consequence of turbulent histories during which cultures, languages, religions and values have come into conflict. Canada is no exception: we can't help seeing that the values, the demands, the political choices of some have a tendency to, at the very least, irritate the others.

And there's nothing especially troubling about this. Love is not a functional basis of operations. It's more of an immature response to a complex problem. Tensions in binational states are normal; the wisest path and the most effective approach consist in accepting those tensions and managing them, rather than denying their existence by means of amorous outbursts.

The Montreal love-in failed to impress me in tactical terms as well. What I saw was a purely narcissistic exercise. English Canadians, arriving in groups, demonstrated with other English Canadians, also in groups, and then took off again by bus, by car or by plane without ever having met the object of their effusions. The true gesture of love would have consisted in saying to Quebecers, "We love you, we don't want to lose you, and here's what we would do so that you could stay" — just as (to revisit interpersonal relationship analogies) a spouse would to prevent a separation. But the message in fact sounded more like this: "Don't leave, because we love Canada the way it is." What Canadians loved, that day, was not French-speaking Quebecers, but themselves.

The third pillar of this new nationalism is, of course, the culture of solidarity that finds expression in the values of sharing, a progressive tax structure, equalization policies and, above all, a social-security safety net of the European type.

The trap does not lie in these admirable policies, but in what they've generated in the collective unconscious. They have served to shape the Canadian identity because they help distinguish Canada from its threatening neighbour.

The result is a Canadian identity that is extremely vulnerable, because the soul of the people comes to depend not on the citizens, not on values, but instead on government programs, on civil servants, on budgets. A budget crisis, or even relatively innocuous acts like closing a railroad link or shutting down a regional radio station, become nation-destroying gestures. There is the concomitant tendency towards a paralysis of choice and of decision-making processes, since every change risks being perceived as an attack on the identity.

This identity attachment, over the years, has crystallized around the health-care system, which has become the symbol par excellence of the Canadian soul, the purest expression of its difference measured against American values. This attachment enshrined itself in a Canadian law on health care that, in the early 1980s, laid out the conditions to which provincial health plans would have to submit. And thus it is that the symbol of identity boils down to a law with five conditions and one formula, almost a mantra: one-tier system.

Not only is this a dogmatic approach, but it removes us from the real world and delivers us to the land of myths. Partly because Canada, despite its attachment to the formula, has never had a truly one-tier system. But mostly because this way of organizing a health-care network exists nowhere else in the industrialized world. Every regime, including those of left-leaning countries in Europe, allows the private and the public to coexist; they accept that not all activities are provided free of charge; they accept that the state shares the management of the system with other partners. What are defined as illegal acts in Canada and perceived as morally reprehensible avenues are accepted in every country that believes in solidarity.

The absolutely surrealistic nature of the thing was made clear to me in all its splendour when the former health minister Allan Rock, with whom I had shared this observation, answered me that, yes, there was in fact a nation whose system rested on the same principles as ours … Cuba. This was not, alas, meant as a joke.

Rigidities That Come with a Price

There's a price to be paid for these rigidities, which entail numerous perverse effects.

There is first of all the fact that they deprive us of the possibility of exploring other avenues of reform. This seems to me to be the case in health care, where the choke-hold that Canada has applied to itself will make the colossal undertaking of re-engineering the health-care system, restoring the quality of care and people's confidence, much more difficult.

Similarly, the ideological framework that the Canadian government has imposed on itself will make challenges more difficult to meet, among them the necessity of raising the standard of living of Canadians and of lessening the gap that is deepening dangerously between us and our neighbour.

Another perverse effect, a much more disquieting one, is the development in Canada of an ideological orthodoxy. In Quebec there are pressures that discourage intellectuals from straying from sovereigntist dogma and thus running the risk of exclusion and mistrust. I know something about this. The same process is at work in Canada, on another basis, that of the Canadian social model. It is difficult to be a true Canadian without espousing the centre-left values that underlie our welfare state.

The idea of then premier of Ontario Bob Rae, when during our great constitutional debates he sought to have social rights enshrined in the Charter, reflects this tendency. The idea was noble and generous. But it carried with it important secondary effects, centring on the fact that for all practical purposes, the elements of a political program whose values are not necessarily universal and certainly not shared by all Canadians would have been constitutionalized.

This homogeneous political vision can also lead to abuse. For example, a federal minister told me that another former premier of Ontario, Mike Harris, was "un-Canadian," which reminds us how easy it is for nationalism to lead to intolerance.

This ideological orthodoxy contributed considerably, in my opinion, to fostering the alienation of the west and the anger against central Canada that found expression in the Reform Party and the Canadian Alliance. In effect, Canadian citizens were deprived of their democratic right, that of being *on* the right, and of expressing, in the organization of their collective life, values that differ from those of the central government. Therein lies a certain democratic deficit.

I do not support the Alliance. But I defend the right to be different, and even the possibility that other roads are capable of enriching our collective experience. And above all, I defend the inalienable right of Canadians to be able to choose.

This leads to another perverse effect that is beginning to appear in the Canadian political landscape. The ideological corridor is narrow to the point where only one political party can still embody the untouchable and unassailable values that define Canada, and that is the Liberal Party of Canada. So much so that Canada is gradually making its way towards a new situation, that of a single-party parliamentary regime.

That is why I fear that Canada is not well prepared for the challenges that the future holds in store, and that its nationalism, and the way in which that nationalism shapes the Canadian identity, risks being an obstacle rather than a positive force for progress.

The Canadian search for identity has, for some decades, instead of liberating Canada and Canadians succeeded in placing us in chains. A questioning of certain myths that are suffocating Canada has therefore become necessary, in order that Canada embrace a nationalism that is positive and creative and that the country have at its disposal the tools it will need in the years that lie ahead.

This is a question that needs to be faced all the more urgently in light of the new types of challenge that Canada will confront, most especially the impact of globalization on economic activity, on the role of states, on the fate of peoples. These pressures, which may turn out to be enormous, will demand from societies like ours — if we wish to resist them and continue to be what we are — strong identities and a great ability to adapt. For the moment, we would have trouble exhibiting either one or the other.

One way of finding that flexibility and ridding ourselves of sacred cows is debate. Canadians reflect all too little, except in specialized circles, on their identity, on the expressions of their nationalism. Taking comfort from their dogma, rocked in the cradle of ideological orthodoxy, Canadians have lost the daring, iconoclastic approach of the man who still inspires them, Pierre Trudeau. A little more reason, a little more lucidity would not harm the Canadian debate.

Another liberating tool is regionalization. I have no wish to talk here about the decentralization of power, or of the workings of federalism — however much I happen to be a supporter of decentralization. I will talk about something deeper, a state of mind, a way of perceiving the Canadian dynamic whereby the regions can play a role as a setting for initiative and for identity definition.

In Canadian history, the initiatives of regions, the competition that takes place among them and imitation have been major factors in national progress. I know there are some who associate modernity with a stronger central role, capable of countering what they see as provincial deviancy. But the regions are a source of creativity and energy that a sclerotic centre with an aging leadership cannot ensure. These regional identities exist in Canada, they are rich, and they should not merely be encouraged but showcased. They should be perceived as factors that enrich the national identity rather than pressures from outside that constitute a threat to it.

Betting on regions seems to me more the order of the day as globalization comes to have a greater impact on the architecture of states, creates networks that transcend the traditional logic of borders and deprives people of frames of reference to which they've grown accustomed. These upheavals tend to lead citizens to reinforce their sense of identity at the regional level. This phenomenon of regional reinforcement, obvious in Europe, will take shape in Canada as free trade imposes a north–south logic. Canada is obviously not prepared to facilitate this process.

To this may be added another pressure linked to globalization, less obvious, more distant, that could be characterized as a long shot but that seems to me to be important to prepare for. And that is the impact of continentalization, which to this point in time has found expression mostly at the economic level.

North America — and soon simply the Americas, with the Free Trade Area of the Americas — lags behind Europe in terms of political integration. But the fact remains that Canadians, and the younger ones especially, will progressively develop what can be called a continental awareness, a certain sense of belonging, a modification of what is their implicit space. The mobility of students, of researchers, of management, the growth of transnational Canadian firms, the circulation of ideas — all this will have the effect that a growing number of Canadians, while remaining Canadians, will be North Americans as well in certain areas of their lives. This can now, unfortunately, be seen in some aspects of cultural life, but in time it will certainly come to affect other components of everyday living.

A new reality will emerge from this process: double identity, the mere evocation of which is bound to produce a shudder in many Canadians. But if the state is complex, it can nonetheless be managed — as we are beginning to see in Europe, where Germans, French and Italians are learning to be European citizens as well. This is something that Quebecers are very familiar with, being Quebecers and Canadians at one and the same time. Someday it will be your turn.

It can work — on the condition, of course, that the national identity is firmly grounded to begin with.

I'm not a specialist on the Canadian question — I'm not even Canadian in the same way that you are, given this double identity of mine. And that could possibly lead me to a degree of oversimplification. But my impression, despite certain misgivings, is that the Canadian identity is strong, in lifestyle, in the attachment to institutions, in values, in behaviours, in certain components of cultural life — much more than Canadian leaders, heirs to and caretakers of cultural insecurity, seem to believe.

The finest example, once again, is that of health care. It is not Jean Chrétien or Joe Clark or Stockwell Day or Gilles Duceppe or Alexa McDonough who is the custodian of the system; rather, it is Canadians themselves, who, without their politicians, have expressed in a thousand ways their objection to seeing a regime of the American type installed in Canada.

The rigidity of Canadian nationalism and of its symbols can be explained in large part by that obligation felt by our elites to furnish a bulwark protecting the Canadian identity. But that identity is strong enough to express itself without the artificial protection that the central power deems it its obligation to supply.

That paternalistic approach can have the opposite effect. In desiring to protect Canadians from themselves, in imposing on Canadians crutches for which they have no need, in instilling in them a sense of insecurity unjustified by reality, the risk is rather that the country as a whole will be enfeebled.

This, in essence, is the message I delivered to my readers in Quebec one year ago. It's a message, I believe, that applies equally well to Canadians, almost word for word.

Georges Erasmus

∼ 3RD ANNUAL
LAFONTAINE-BALDWIN LECTURE

The Fairmont Hotel Vancouver
Vancouver, British Columbia
Friday, March 8, 2002

Introduction

I am honoured by the invitation to contribute to the LaFontaine-Baldwin lecture series, imagining the kind of Canada we want in the twenty-first century. And I welcome the opportunity to reflect with you on the issues that we need to address in order to realize that vision.

To paint a picture of the Canada that Aboriginal people envision, I need only turn to the ideals of a good life embedded in Aboriginal languages and traditional teachings. The Anishinabek seek the spiritual gift of *pimatziwin* — long life and well-being that enable a person to gain wisdom. The Cree of the northern prairies value *miyowicehtowin* — having good relations. The Iroquois Great Law sets out rules for maintaining peace, *Skennen kowa,* among peoples, going beyond resolving conflicts to actively caring for each other's welfare. Aboriginal peoples across Canada internationally speak of their relationship with the natural world and the responsibility of human beings to maintain balance in the natural order. Rituals in which we give something back in return for the gifts that we receive from Mother Earth reinforce that sense of responsibility.

I would guess that most Canadians subscribe to these same goals: long life, health and wisdom for self and family; a harmonious and cohesive society; peace among peoples of different origins and territories; and a sustainable relationship with the natural environment. Canadians would probably also agree in principle with the traditional Aboriginal ethic that our actions today should not jeopardize the health, peace and well-being of generations yet unborn.

If there is such a convergence of basic values between Aboriginal and non-Aboriginal peoples, why is communication between us so difficult, so riddled with misunderstandings and tension?

There is a problem of language. A study done for the Royal Commission on Aboriginal Peoples examined over two hundred commission and task force reports issued between 1966 and 1991. The researchers pointed out that even when we used the same words, Aboriginal people and government representatives were often talking about different things. The research also traced remarkable consistency in the issues and positions that Aboriginal peoples were articulating over those twenty-five years. I will return again to the issue of historical continuity in Aboriginal peoples' priorities. I first want to focus on the nature of discourse between our cultures. By discourse, I mean the way we carry on conversations.

Intercultural discourse is carried on predominantly in English or French. Since this requires translation of concepts and experience, there is the normal problem of finding words in a second language that approximate the meaning we want to convey. But beyond that, the discourse has been framed in terms that are often fundamentally alien to the way we think about an issue. Take "land claims," for example. Elders in our nations find it strange that younger leaders launch "claims" to lands that have supported our peoples since time immemorial. "Comprehensive and specific claims" are the terms around which the government of Canada is prepared to engage in legalistic dialogue. Aboriginal peoples have had to work with the prescribed terms in order to get land questions on the policy agenda, even though the language distorts our reality. The discourse is driven by an imbalance in power and considerations of strategy. In other areas as well — governance, health, education — Aboriginal peoples have been required to adopt language that is not quite our own.

I want to take most of this hour to suggest how dialogue with Aboriginal peoples might be framed in different terms, looking for language that expresses Aboriginal perspectives and also connects with the aspirations of a wide spectrum of Canadians.

Creating and sustaining a national community is an ongoing act of imagination, fuelled by stories of who we are. The narratives of how Canada came to be are only now beginning to acknowledge the fundamental contributions that Aboriginal peoples have made to the formation of Canada as we know it. We were major participants in the trade and commerce that supported settlement. We were partners in the treaty-making that opened access to lands and resources. We were in the front lines protecting Canadian borders in 1812–14. And we volunteered in extraordinary numbers in World War I and World War II to defend democratic values overseas. We are convinced that we also bring something of value as Aboriginal peoples to meeting the political and economic challenges that Canada faces in this new century.

If that contribution is to be fully realized, we need to engage in conversations that go beyond policy debates with govern- ments. We need to talk "people to people" as well as "nation to nation."

I propose to try shifting the terms of discourse along three lines: from Aboriginal rights to relationship between peoples; from crying needs to vigorous capacity; from individual citizen- ship to nations within the nation-state.

Aboriginal Rights: Relationship between Peoples

Aboriginal rights seriously entered the vocabulary of Canadian law and public policy in 1973, when a Supreme Court judgment acknowledged that the Nisga'a of British Columbia had Aboriginal title to their traditional lands, based on their use and occupancy of those lands from time immemorial. The Nisga'a had never entered into treaties with the British colonial govern- ment or Canada. Members of the court were divided on whether enactments of federal and provincial law had extinguished Nisga'a title. Resolution of the Nisga'a land question would not be achieved until the signing of a treaty in 1998.

Aboriginal and treaty rights gained protection in the Canadian Constitution of 1982 with the provision that "the existing aboriginal and treaty rights of the aboriginal peoples of Canada are hereby recognized and affirmed." A series of Supreme Court decisions has given some definition of how these rights are to be interpreted under Canadian law, but there has never been a negotiated agreement between Aboriginal nations and Canada on the nature of these rights. Each court decision addresses a portion of the larger issue, raising a host of new questions. The Marshall decision of 1999 affirming Mi'kmaq rights, under a 1760 treaty, to earn a moderate living from the Atlantic fishery did not put an end to disputes about how resources are to be shared.

Gaining recognition of Aboriginal rights in the courts and entrenchment in the Constitution have been critical to restoring Aboriginal peoples as active agents in directing our collective lives. Where land claims settlements have proceeded, they have opened possibilities for social, cultural, political and economic renewal. But there have been some unfortunate side effects of the rights agenda. An American Indian law professor has written that "like other minority groups in our society, tribal Indians must demonstrate a convergence of their interests with dominant group interests in promoting their rights." This is difficult because "the rights they claim seem so alien and opposed to the dominant society's legal, political, and cultural traditions."

Aboriginal rights have been delineated in the context of long, contentious court cases in which Aboriginal interests have been pitted against Canadian state parties who are purportedly representing the public interest. Legal scholars and constitutional experts, standing within the Canadian legal system, interpret what Aboriginal peoples want and what obligations rest with Canadian governments to accede to those claims.

Litigation is no way to build a community! It is not the way preferred by Aboriginal peoples. We have a history of treaty-making that stretches back long before Columbus. Drawing on those traditions, through two centuries of expanding settlement, the Mi'kmaq, Mohawk, Ojibwa, Saulteaux, Cree, Dene and other Aboriginal nations sat down in councils and entered treaty negotiations to discuss how to establish good relations with newcomers. This is how Canada came to be a "peaceable kingdom," not one born of violence and conquest. A non-Aboriginal scholar working with the royal commission, who had spent years of his life researching treaty history, declared, "These are my treaties too. They legitimize my place in this land."

Aboriginal treaties are often described in legal terms as creating a *trust relationship,* one that invests the trustee with superior power and greater ethical responsibilities. For Aboriginal peoples, treaties created a *relationship of mutual trust* that was sacred and enduring. The bond created was like that of brothers who might have different gifts and follow different paths, but who could be counted on to render assistance to one another in times of need.

Renewing the relationship between Aboriginal and non-Aboriginal peoples in Canada is the major theme of the 1996 *Report of the Royal Commission on Aboriginal Peoples.* The RCAP report presented a comprehensive set of recommendations to restore a relationship of mutual trust, starting with an acknowledgement of historic wrongs, a ceremonial commitment to renewing the relationship and the establishment of laws and institutions to ensure that commitments would be acted upon.

It is now more than five years since RCAP reported to the prime minister and the people of Canada. There is a consensus among Aboriginal peoples, scholars and activists that little has changed in the interim. Underlying tensions over lands and treaty rights continue to boil up into open conflict. Litigation on residential schools wends its slow and tortuous way through the courts, bringing satisfaction and closure to no one. The federal minister of Indian Affairs has unilaterally announced a timetable for consultations and revisions to the Indian Act, without regard to the advice of RCAP that Aboriginal consent is essential to a renewed relationship.

In the months following the armed confrontation between Mohawks and Canadian authorities at Oka, there was an urgent and audible demand from the Canadian public to repair the relationship that had gone visibly wrong. In the decade since Oka, that sense of urgency appears to have subsided. Polling data indicate that there is still public support for spending to resolve social problems and, to a lesser degree, support for self-government and the cultural survival of Aboriginal peoples. The framing of the questions solicits answers that reinforce a sense of distance and reluctant obligation. Aboriginal peoples, guided by their traditions, would pose other questions: In this situation, how can we establish good relations? In the circle of our relations, how do we maintain harmony and well-being?

We have not found a way to ignite the imagination of contemporary Canadians with the possibilities represented in the Kaswentah, the wampum belt recording eighteenth-century treaties between the Iroquois and the colonists that has struck a responsive chord with other Aboriginal nations. The Kaswentah shows the wake of two vessels, a First Nations canoe and a European sailing ship travelling together on the river of life. The peoples represented retain their own identity and autonomy, but they are linked to one another by principles of truth, respect and friendship. The two-row wampum belt is often read as a symbol of separateness. In fact, it symbolizes a strong, ethical relationship between peoples.

Aboriginal Needs, Aboriginal Capacity

Perhaps one of the impediments to the mutual relationship envisioned by Aboriginal peoples is the notion that we are an exceptionally needy population. The picture of needs blocks out a perception of Aboriginal capacity. I suspect that media images of gas-sniffing youth in Davis Inlet are etched in the memories of most adult Canadians. There are other Aboriginal communities where substance abuse and clusters of suicide and suicidal behaviour are at crisis proportions. But there is also evidence from many quarters that Aboriginal peoples are in the midst of a remarkable resurgence — in education, healing and community wellness, the arts and economic activity.

Considering the primary importance of children in Aboriginal cultures it is not surprising that education was one of the first sectors where Aboriginal nations and communities moved to reassert control over their lives. Many schools in First Nations communities are now administered locally, and where possible they incorporate Aboriginal languages and cultural content in the curriculum. More youth are staying in school to complete a high school diploma, though a gap still exists between graduation rates of Aboriginal and non-Aboriginal young people. Post-secondary enrolments of registered Indian students have held steady at around 22,500 nationally for the past five years. The most remarkable fact about this group of students is that the largest proportion of them (42 percent) is over thirty years of age. The pattern is that Aboriginal students leave school as youth and return as adults, often with family responsibilities, to complete academic and vocational credentials.

Re-entry into post-secondary education has become more attractive with the introduction of Native studies and

Aboriginal-specific programs in colleges and universities across the country. Aboriginal faculty are establishing a growing presence as role models, mentors and instructors. Aboriginal colleges and institutes have also become major players in post secondary education. A few, like Saskatchewan Indian Federated College and the Nicola Valley Institute of Technology in British Columbia, offer provincially recognized diploma and degree programs. Most of the forty-three Aboriginal institutes across Canada have partnership arrangements with accredited provincial colleges and universities. The institutes, under Aboriginal control, are helping to narrow the gap in educational attainment by developing and delivering community-based, culturally relevant programs, serving adult students as well as youth.

Aboriginal initiatives in healing and wellness, like those in education, are showing high levels of effectiveness. Research is confirming that Aboriginal services are also cost-efficient.

Community Holistic Circle Healing was initiated in Hollow Water, Manitoba, in response to alarming incidents of sexual abuse, including abuse of children. Berma Bushie, one of the key participants in the strategy, described the situation facing the community in 1987: "The child welfare and legal system were at our door. The community had no involvement. Offenders were sent to jail where they had to deny their offence to survive, and two or three years later they were turned back into the community to offend again."

The thirteen-step program of intervention pioneered at Hollow Water engages the whole community, along with victims of abuse, offenders and their families, in assuming responsibility for restoring safety, health and balance.

In 2001 the ministry of the Solicitor General for Canada and the Aboriginal Healing Foundation sponsored a cost-benefit analysis of ten years' experience with Community Holistic Circle Healing. Over a ten-year period, federal and provincial ministries contributed $2.4 million to the project. A total of 107 offenders who acknowledged their offences were dealt with. The research calculated that for each two dollars of investment by federal and provincial ministries, the return was between six and sixteen dollars in services rendered in lieu of pre-incarceration, prison, probation and parole. These figures reflect the efficiencies achieved through community-led services that would otherwise have been provided by government agencies. The analysis does not take into account that the rate of reoffending over the ten-year period was less than 2 percent for offenders in Circle Healing, while estimated rates of recidivism are 13 percent for sex offences and 36 percent for other offences. Neither does this very conservative cost analysis account for benefits to the community that include improvements reported in child health, better parenting skills, increased safety and community responsibility overall. As a footnote, although residential school experience and its intergenerational effects are significantly implicated in the offences treated by Circle Healing, not one legal action had been filed by a Hollow Water community member as a result of residential school abuse.

Evidence is accumulating that Aboriginal organizations are very effective in mobilizing human resources to meet challenges. The Aboriginal Healing Foundation was established in 1998 to distribute $350 million allocated by the federal government to address the effects of physical and sexual abuse in residential schools. Many Aboriginal people who attended residential schools, or whose parents attended residential schools, experience post-traumatic stress, suicide attempts and life-threatening addictions, among other expressions of need. The Foundation has committed and distributed $156 million to community-based healing in the form of eight hundred grants. In June 2001 an interim evaluation surveyed just over three hundred of the projects funded to date. The survey found that 1,686 communities and communities of interest were being served; just under fifty-nine thousand Aboriginal people were engaged in healing projects, less than 1 percent of whom had been involved in healing previously; and almost eleven thousand Aboriginal people were receiving training as a result of funded projects. In an average month, thirteen thousand hours of volunteer service in the community were logged. Program investments are having a multiplier effect unheard of in government services.

Right across Canada, alternative justice projects, healing circles and Aboriginal agencies are reaching out and drawing angry, alienated, despairing individuals back into the circle of the community, where they discover their worth as human beings, recognize their relationships and begin to make their unique contribution to community well-being.

Aboriginal arts and artists are playing an important part in the revitalization of the Aboriginal community. They are also making their mark in society at large. Aboriginal superstars have been around for a long time: Buffy Sainte-Marie and her presence at the Academy Awards and on *Sesame Street;* Bill Reid bringing Haida art forms to national prominence; Douglas Cardinal as the architect of the Museum of Civilization. We now have another generation of artists and writers giving expression to their Aboriginal identity and experience with eloquence and humour: Eden Robinson, a Haisla author, was nominated last year for both the Giller Prize and the Governor General's Award for fiction for her first novel, *Monkey Beach;* Tomson Highway has received international recognition as an author and playwright; Drew Hayden Taylor writes television scripts as well as plays and humorous columns. When Aboriginal people, especially youth, see Susan Aglukark on the music charts and Graham Greene in the movies, the range of scripts for their own lives is expanded. It was cause for celebration in February this year when an Inuit film, *Atanarjuat (The Fast Runner)*, swept the Genie Awards, winning a total of six categories, including Best Picture, Best Direction and Best Screenplay.

The Aboriginal Peoples' Television Network, which began broadcasting in 1999, represents a huge step forward in Aboriginal arts and communications. APTN grew out of regional Aboriginal broadcasting initiatives, particularly the Inuit Broadcasting Corporation and Northern Native Broadcasting Network. It provides multiple lenses through which Aboriginal people can see the world and themselves and by which the public at large can view public affairs, community activities and cultural programming through Aboriginal eyes. APTN's influence is being extended as it partners with other agencies to produce and distribute a variety of programs, which, in turn, are broadcast on regional outlets.

I have mentioned that land claims settlements have opened economic opportunities for some Aboriginal communities. Development projects funded through government programs or private-sector partnerships are having an impact on others. I want to highlight the activity of Aboriginal entrepreneurs as another expression of Aboriginal capacity.

A 1996 survey by Statistics Canada identified over twenty thousand Aboriginal-owned businesses. This represents a three-fold increase between 1981 and 1996. Forty-six percent of these businesses have at least one additional full-time, permanent employee. The numbers of Aboriginal women and Metis owners are showing the fastest growth. Businesses are concentrated in the primary sectors of fishing, trapping and farming, along with the contracting trades, but Aboriginal owners are also represented in a wide variety of enterprises, including management consulting, software design, manufacturing and tourism. These figures on entrepreneurship do not include community-owned businesses, which typically operate on a larger scale and set goals to promote training, employment and community economic development along with profit-making. Meadow Lake Tribal Council Forest Industries is a highly successful enterprise in the resource sector. Air Creebec and First Air, started with capital from claims settlements, are thriving in the highly competitive airline industry.

Despite the resurgence in Aboriginal capacity in the past thirty years, the gap between Aboriginal and general Canadian life opportunities remains disturbingly wide. While Canada regularly ranks first on the United Nations index for quality of life, registered Indians living on-reserve would rank sixty-third and registered Indians on- and off-reserve would rank forty-seventh after applying the UN criteria of education, income and life expectancy. Young Aboriginals are especially vulnerable. They are less likely than mature adults to have attained academic and vocational credentials, and they are hit hardest by unemployment. Moving from a reserve or rural settlement to the city improves income and employment prospects, but only marginally.

Strategies for building on Aboriginal capacity have been set out in the RCAP report and in subsequent forums. They include supporting community-led initiatives that mobilize Aboriginal people in diverse situations to deal with their own issues; creating space for Aboriginal institutions that provide sustained, effective leadership in accord with the culture of the community; promoting partnerships and collaboration among Aboriginal people, the private sector and public institutions to break down isolation and barriers to productive relationships; and recognizing the authority of Aboriginal nations to negotiate the continuing place of Aboriginal peoples in Canadian society, whether on their traditional lands or in the city.

Citizenship as Individuals: Nations within the Nation-State

For most of the years since the first Indian Act was passed in 1876, being Aboriginal or "Indian" was perceived to be incompatible with being a Canadian citizen. When the option of enfranchisement, trading Indian status for voting rights, failed to attract individuals, more coercive measures were enacted, enfranchising Indians if they lived away from their reserves, joined the military, obtained higher education or, in the case of women, if they married a non-Indian. The object of policy, baldly stated in 1920 by Duncan Campbell Scott, superintendent of Indian Affairs, was "to continue until there is not a single Indian in Canada that has not been absorbed into the body politic and there is no Indian question and no Indian Department." The same object was reflected in the 1969 White Paper, which proposed, in the language of democracy, to make Indians "citizens like any other." The response of Aboriginal peoples to all these attempts to "break them into pieces" has been consistent resistance. Aboriginal proposals for a nation-to-nation relationship have proven problematic in attempted dialogue with governments and with Canadians at large. I want to spend a few minutes reframing the discourse on nation identities.

My first point is that Aboriginal peoples have maintained our identities as nations since time immemorial. As nations we made treaties with one another, with European emissaries and the Crown in right of Canada. As nations we have successfully asserted our rights before Canadian courts to enjoy benefits from our traditional lands. In negotiations leading to the failed Charlottetown Accord on the Constitution, we won reluctant acknowledgement from Canadian governments that Aboriginal self-government is an inherent right, not a privilege granted by other authority.

It seems to us that the continuing existence of Aboriginal nations is a political and legal reality as well as a historical fact. How that reality is accommodated in relations with the Canadian state and Canadian people is a matter for negotiation. I would simply say to you that we can't begin a dialogue on building a future together if the conversation starts with the unilateral declaration "You are not who you say you are!"

My second point is that most of the thorny issues raised as impediments to nation-to-nation relations have been confronted and resolved in the treaty concluded in 1998 by the Nisga'a Nation, Canada and British Columbia. The treaty secures to the Nisga'a control of a portion of their traditional territory and a share of natural resources in other areas. It frees up vast areas of Nisga'a homelands for use and development by Canada, British Columbia and commercial interests. The treaty deals with Nisga'a legislative powers, government-to-government fiscal transfers and taxation.

I'm not proposing that the Nisga'a treaty should be a template for nation-to-nation relations, but it does provide an example of how a practical agreement can be put in place without undermining the integrity of the Canadian federation.

My final point on nation-to-nation relations concerns the practical benefits to Aboriginal peoples and to Canada of recognizing and accommodating the authority of Aboriginal nations. Stable Aboriginal governments with recognized jurisdiction, resources to implement decisions and legitimacy in the eyes of citizens can achieve social and economic renewal more effectively than federal and provincial governments have been able to do. The evidence is in.

The Harvard Project on American Indian Economic Development reported in 1992 on research in fifty ventures over a five-year period. The project attempted to determine why economic ventures in some tribes succeed and in others fail. The findings, confirmed in subsequent studies, showed that effective governance is a critical factor in fostering economic development. The characteristics of effective government were identified as 1) having power to make decisions about a community's own future; 2) exercising power through effective institutions; and 3) choosing economic policies and projects that fit with values and priorities, that is, the culture of the community.

The findings on economic development in American Indian tribes are mirrored in a World Bank study of 1998 that found a negative correlation between foreign aid and growth. The study raised doubts about the assumption that injections of capital from abroad would be the main way of achieving significant social and economic benefits in developing countries. Having effective government institutions at the community level that support sound economic policies and inclusive social policy is far more influential than previously understood.

Recognizing nations and establishing institutions to implement the inherent right of self-government are important, but they are not sufficient to enable Aboriginal people to thrive in

Canada. The Royal Commission on Aboriginal Peoples pointed out that political gains will be hollow without the economic means to sustain them. The economic base for many Aboriginal nations is to be found in the potential for wealth standing on, lying under or flowing through their traditional territories.

The United Nations Human Rights Committee took up the theme of lands and resources in its 1999 review of Canada's compliance with the UN Covenant on Civil and Political Rights. The Committee challenged Canada in these words:

> With reference to the conclusion by RCAP that without a greater share of lands and resources institutions of aboriginal self-government will fail, the Committee emphasizes that the right to self-determination requires, *inter alia,* that all peoples must be able to freely dispose of their natural wealth and resources and that they may not be deprived of their own means of subsistence. The Committee recommends that decisive and urgent action be taken towards the full implementation of the RCAP recommendations on land and resource allocation.

The Future Begins Now

As I was in the final stages of preparing this talk, I was anticipating the questions that might be stimulated by this vision of building a common future. Can we get there from here? What are the costs? Is it in the public interest of Canada as a whole?

At the same time, a historic event was taking place in northern Quebec. In February, the Grand Council of the

Crees and Premier Bernard Landry signed a nation-to-nation agreement to guide development in the region over the next fifty years. The agreement sets a new standard for securing the consent of an Aboriginal nation to development on its lands. It provides for sharing of resource revenue from three sectors: electricity, mining and forestry; and it recognizes the Cree people's right to determine their own economic future.

Grand Chief Ted Moses, in his speech at the signing ceremony, answered many of the questions I was thinking about. He said, in part:

> For twenty-six years the Cree Nation has been fighting to breathe life and spirit into [the James Bay and Northern Quebec Agreement] that has become the subject of many legal challenges — challenges from the Crees, challenges from the governments and from others.
>
> Today we will be able to put that adversity behind us, and redirect our attention, our energy, and our imaginations to our common effort, in real partnership with Quebec, to plan for a future that includes Les Québécois, includes the Cree People.... The agreement we are signing here today ... is the first serious step in the implementation of the recommendations of the Royal Commission on Aboriginal Peoples, and is, for now, the *only* instance in Canada of a governmental authority recognizing and implementing the operational principles of self-determination called for by the United Nations Human Rights Committee.

I have argued that a new relationship between Aboriginal peoples and others in Canada is urgently needed, that it will bring benefit to both Aboriginal and non-Aboriginal partners, that it is consistent with Canadian law and social values.

There is another compelling reason to join our efforts to achieve good relations. The world needs a model of peace and friendship between peoples that Canada is uniquely positioned to provide.

The greatest challenge to the world community in this century is how to promote harmonious relations among peoples of disparate origins, histories, languages and religions who find themselves intermingled in a single state. The U.S.S.R. has fractured into constituent nations. The former Yugoslavia has fallen into bitter strife along nationalist and religious lines. The troubles in Northern Ireland continue to flare up in spite of international efforts to broker peace.

Canada and Canadians have played a prominent and distinguished role in advancing the philosophy, practice and protection of human rights around the world. Michael Ignatieff, in a recent book, cites Canada's remarkable inventiveness in finding ways to enable a large, multi-ethnic, multinational state to survive and even prosper. Negotiation and compromise were instituted as civic values in the historic alliance of anglophones and francophones led by Baldwin and LaFontaine in 1848. But before that, Aboriginal peoples had introduced warring Europeans to the protocols by which nations could relate to one another as brothers, travelling the river of life sharing prosperity and hardship, autonomous enough to guide their own vessels but close enough to render mutual aid.

Public discourse on relations with Aboriginal peoples has been overtaken by inertia in recent years. The issues that flare up periodically within Canada and mar Canada's reputation as a human rights advocate internationally will not disappear on their own. The words of Zebedee Nungak, an Inuit leader, speaking in the final moments of a First Ministers' meeting in 1987, ring true for many Aboriginal people today:

> We continue to have a hope that this great country, which we embrace as our own, will have the sense and the decency — not that I doubt its decency — to someday, in my generation, recognize our rights, and complete the circle of Confederation, because if it is not going to be done in my generation, I have my son standing behind me who will take up the fight with your sons and your sons' sons.

The costs of conflict, in the courts and in society, are unsupportable. The costs of doing nothing escalate with each generation. We have the capacity to imagine a better future and we have the tools at hand to realize it. Let us decide now to pursue our common goals together, to achieve long life, health and wisdom for all, good relations and peace among peoples and respect for the earth that supports us.

Masi cho. Thank you for your attention.

～ CONVERSATION ONE

RUDYARD GRIFFITHS: Let's start by discussing the future of the concepts of democracy and citizenship. In your respective lectures, it seems that these notions of citizenship and civic agency are being challenged. They're being challenged by globalism, by consumerism, by nationalism. And I'm wondering if the three of you can comment on where you see citizenship going. Is the model envisaged by LaFontaine and Baldwin of the engaged kind of egalitarian citizen still viable in Canada? Is it a model we need to rethink or change? And what are the obstacles to an open, active and thoughtful practice of citizenship in Canada today? Who would like to start?

ALAIN DUBUC: I will. I think that citizenship is a relative concept, not an absolute one. Citizenship is about common values, but it's also about identity, and this is not something that was thought about in the past. Obviously, we see it burgeoning with the French, and we also now see it with immigrants who do not so readily accept shedding their culture when they arrive in

Canada. So we have to deal with the fact that new Canadians won't be Canadian in the same way; they won't see Canada in the same way. That's one problem.

The second problem is that some people will have multiple identities and so will be Canadian in their own way. This is true for the French and it will also be true for new Canadians. Probably the notion of identity will evolve for Canadians, the classical English-speaking Canadians themselves, in relation to the different parts of the country they inhabit and in relation to the world. Are they North American? Are they world citizens? And in the way we see all countries evolve, I think that we have to deal with a kind of puzzle where nobody will be able to define themselves as a Canadian.

RUDYARD GRIFFITHS: So no one will have an exclusive licence on citizenship.

JOHN RALSTON SAUL: When I go out and talk to people, I sense an enormous frustration in citizens, and it has many sounds: an Aboriginal is frustrated, a francophone is frustrated, a new Canadian is frustrated. Nobody is talking to them about how they're going to be citizens and how they're going to fit in. People feel that there isn't really a role for them to play except to vote, or very, very minimal participation. In terms of decisions that are going to be made — the major decisions — you can't say much. The small decisions you might have an impact on. So there's a central question. Are we going to find a positive way to be citizens, or are we going to be reactive and angry? What you're starting to see in Europe is an increasing rise of anger among the citizens who feel left out. You can see that happening politically throughout Europe in a very serious way.

On the other hand, Canada, since it arose from a relatively intellectual idea of how to put together a country, actually isn't a bad foundation from which to think about being a citizen in the future. We accept that you can have group rights, you can have individual rights, et cetera. The hard part is that we have to be linked together by a concept of what holds us together, as opposed to race or language or region. We can also have all those things, or any variety of them. I actually think Canadians are quite comfortable with this idea of citizenship as a hand of cards.

I'll put it slightly differently. It's as if everybody knows they've got a hand of cards — you're a Dene, you're from the Northwest Territories, you're a Canadian — and they can just go down this list and play any card at any time, or any number of cards at any time. Canadians are comfortable with that, but I'm not sure that the formal structures are comfortable with it.

GEORGES ERASMUS: I think that because Canada as a country is still very young, there's a lot of growth that's still going to happen. The influence from Aboriginal people in the country is still just starting to be felt. The characteristics of the major institutions are mainly non-Aboriginal: they're hierarchical, they create power imbalances. I suspect that as time goes on, you're going to find that with Nunavut and other parts of the Northwest Territories, the Yukon, perhaps the Prairie provinces and so forth, you're going to get some structures that are less hierarchical and you're going to create situations where the values are more influenced by Aboriginal people.

I strongly agree that there will continue to be people that identify more strongly with regions — like Newfoundland or

Quebec or the Dene area of the Northwest Territories — so they will consider themselves that before they call themselves Canadians.

This experiment that we're all involved in is still very young, but we're bringing in new people all the time, and a lot of these people continue to be citizens of the places they came from. We've even seen in the past couple of decades people leaving here to go and join struggles back in their homelands....

RUDYARD GRIFFITHS: Yugoslavia is a good example.

GEORGES ERASMUS: Yes, they might run for office over there, that kind of thing. So you're going to continue to have that kind of dual citizenship, with Canadians remaining citizens elsewhere. But even within Canada, I've always thought that if we were prepared to look at the Quebec question with a bit more openness, we would easily see the people in Quebec being citizens of Quebec first and then citizens of Canada, and it would play really nicely to what Aboriginal people have been trying to get the country to consider for quite some time. The Aboriginal people want to continue to maintain their nationhood. So their citizens would be citizens of their own nation as well as citizens of Canada.

An idea we proposed in the *Report of the Royal Commission on Aboriginal Peoples* [1996] was kind of interesting. We suggested that one of the ways this might be addressed would be carrying passports that first recognize that you're a citizen of the particular nation you're from — a Dene or a Cree or a Nisga'a — and then the Canadian passport, which you could also use.

This would make it possible for many Aboriginal people to start looking at Canada in a different way. We still have many Aboriginal people who will tell you they're not Canadian. The same is true in Quebec, as you know very well. But unless we have the opportunity sometime down the road for this to be addressed, we will continue to have this discussion.

There is definitely something we're all doing together as Canadians. The evolution of our character is not mature, not by any means, and that's partly the reason why we feel so imbalanced all the time. We seem to be knocked over fairly quickly with any kind of strong leanings. You know, we're on the defensive about Quebec, we're defensive about Aboriginal people.

We're bringing in new people, but how do we identify ourselves? We're not American. But we don't need to identify ourselves in the negative, as if we don't know who we are and say what we're not. And I suspect that the growth we're going to go through is going to be quite profound. In the next fifty years, we will start to see the end of some of the issues involving Aboriginal people, and maybe even those in Quebec. When these kinds of issues are actually challenged and dealt with, we can get to another stage.

RUDYARD GRIFFITHS: Let's talk about what that other stage might be. Your Excellency, in your speech ...

JOHN RALSTON SAUL: But just before, I do think that if you're looking at mechanisms, you have to be very conscious that you only have a certain number of mechanisms in any society. And about the only fully functioning mechanism we have that allows new Canadians to join in in some way, and different kinds of Canadians to join in with each other in some way, is the public education system, because most of the others have been severely weakened. Now that's not actually true, because you can stand back and say that there are nation structures among Aboriginals that might be smaller, so they could actually act the way a city state acted in the past, and you'll find all sorts of exceptions such as that. Take Lac St-Jean, Quebec, for example. It's small enough in population that people can feel they're part of an identifiable community. But the vast majority of the population have difficulty finding structures that allow them to have a discussion with themselves. The only time when you can really give citizens an idea of how they fit together is during those first twelve years of school, and then maybe the next four years if they go to university. I think that if a country like Canada loses or endangers that basic principle of universal public education in any way, it will be virtually impossible to make any of what we're discussing work. It would just fly apart, because there would be nothing that could feed the different parts in together.

Rudyard Griffiths: Let's talk about that, and, Alain, maybe you can comment. How do we hold it together? We understand the importance of these multiple identities, as you've said, the need to give them articulation and expression, but we need some kind of support, or a series of supports, to bring that common project of expressing multiple identities together. Coming from Quebec, where do you see, outside of Quebec, those supports that will hold Quebec in the country but will allow for, in a sense, a multiple identity to emerge and to be validated?

Alain Dubuc: It depends. When we talk about situations, we also talk about identity, and identity is defined by the state and by some institutions. It's also defined by values, and what I'm slowly learning about Canada and Quebec is that people hold some strong values, stronger than those put forward by governments and institutions. We see, in the negative way, how Canadians do not want to be, and at least that's a sign that there's a will to do something. I don't think that the way it's expressed is always useful, but I'd like to make a simple acknowledgement that different Canadians can be Canadian in different ways. And if the Canadian model were more eclectic, there would be fewer problems.

John Ralston Saul: I don't know, Georges, what you hear around the country, but one of the most common lines you hear in Nunavut is people basically saying, "We're Canadians now," and what they mean by that is that they are Canadians by choice after the agreement on Nunavut. And it's an extremely positive statement, because they actually have a definition of themselves as Canadians that they're happy with. I don't know if you hear that said, positively or negatively.

Georges Erasmus: Well, the places where you would hear it negatively would be where, for instance, issues have not been resolved — treaties have not been settled, old treaties need to be revisited, land claims have not happened — where the issues still need to be clarified. It's going to be a challenge for that to be seriously addressed, but it can be addressed.

John Ralston Saul: I think if you look at that, and if you look at what Alain is saying, what's interesting is that something like public education is not an institution that tells you what to do. It's not supposed to, at any rate. It's supposed to be an institution in which you can express yourself. It's difficult, but people can meet and things can happen. It's not an institution that is supposed to make everybody into the same thing — at least in Canada, it's not supposed to.

But there is no question that we have a lot of trouble accommodating the differences people are happy with, along with the values that they actually share. That's the thing that strikes me, going across the country. People are very happy in all the things that make them different — it's a positive to them. And they are also very happy that they share these other things that tend to be more abstract, abstract in the sense that they're a value, an idea, an approach that fits into whatever the differences are. The problem is to find a way of expressing that.

ALAIN DUBUC: It's the problem that Baldwin and LaFontaine were aware of. Not only that, but they were able to say so at the same time in our history — they were able to capture common values, or at least the common goals. And if there's a problem — if people have problems expressing their situation — then if politics redefines itself in some way …

RUDYARD GRIFFITHS: Your Excellency, in your speech you said you see a problem with the NGO community, in that it takes on some of the impetus for the articulation of values, and discussions of values, but then it acts entirely outside of Parliament and the democratic process.

JOHN RALSTON SAUL: You know, when I said that, that was actually the first time I'd ever said it and I expected to be stoned. In that hall I think there were probably 50 percent of the people who belonged to one NGO or another, and they seemed to be nodding. I think that people in the NGO community know that, on the one hand, it was and still is a very valid position to be outside of the mainstream of politics on whatever issue interests you, but that at some point the discussion has to bleed into, integrate into the mainstream political parties, start parties, go into parties, go into the mainstream political debate, because otherwise you are siphoning off energy from the mainstream political debate. How does a citizen support a reform, which after all needs to become a law, or an administration or a policy? How do they do that if there's nobody going into mainstream politics to represent it, if everybody's outside?

What you end up doing is treating politics as if it were at another level; in other words, we all stand outside and lobby, and then we sort of beg. We say, "Well, we're the majority, we're ethically right, we beg you to do something." But we haven't actually expressed our majority fully through the electoral process. It's problematic in terms of citizenship.

I'm not suggesting people leave the NGOs. Again, one can be two or three or four things at once. But there is no question that if one looks at the cities, and the people who make up the middle class, which still represents a majority in the country, a lot of people have lost the habit of soiling themselves by getting involved in the political process. Only one of the three of us here has really run for office seriously — Georges. It's a tough process.

Rudyard Griffiths: And, Georges, what's your feeling in terms of the Aboriginal community, the great pressure obviously in that community to act outside of existing parliamentary and regulatory structures because of the sense of frustration and slow pace of reform? Do you think there is still a future for Aboriginals articulating your sense of the public good within the existing framework, political and democratic?

GEORGES ERASMUS: Well, the whole issue of Aboriginal participation in the electoral process in Canada is all caught up in the understood relationship: it either exists or doesn't exist. Again, it comes back to the roots of whether Aboriginal people consider themselves Canadians, and certain ones do not. In central Canada a majority simply say no. The Iroquois Confederacy in large parts of Ontario never entered into that kind of a relationship. So until you resolve those things, the problem is that decade after decade goes by without these issues being addressed. It even extends to the Indian Act elections, where that whole concept of the Band Council was forced on Aboriginal people. Some people took to it, but many didn't, and so you still see, among the Iroquois communities in particular, only small portions of the population who bother to be involved in the elections, because as far as they are concerned it's still an imposed government and it shouldn't be the model. Until we resolve those things, I don't think you're going to have full participation.

But out west and up north, a lot of Aboriginal people will participate, and over time, with numbers changing, more and more of the ridings there are being influenced, and our people are being elected.

We have the example of the Nunavut experience where we now have a territory where the Aboriginal people wanted their own homeland, so they are participating fully there in huge,

huge turnouts. It shows that if you actually do address what the Aboriginal people want, they definitely will get involved.

JOHN RALSTON SAUL: And if you add to that Nunavik, northern Quebec, and now the Cree-Quebec agreement and the Nisga'a agreement, you see that there are big pockets of what could turn into a buy-in in the full sense.

But you know, I often think that what's missing in our discussion — because we're so often talking about ourselves in terms of what we aren't — is that we don't talk enough about the kinds of contributions that areas or groups have made to the national whole. Alain, in our discussions, you talked about the unconsciousness of anglophone Canadians, not knowing they're nationalistic and thinking other people are too nationalistic and not being able to see themselves. Georges, you talked about imagining an instance of actually coming to terms with the contribution that Aboriginals made over four hundred and some years to the way the country works, because we're in denial about the shape of our democracy and where that comes from.

We really have to stop saying that we're a British parliamentary democracy with a British justice system or a French justice system. We have to stop talking in those sorts of nonsense terms and start actually looking at the way our democratic system runs, for better and worse. When you start doing that, you start seeing that there has been enormous input over hundreds of years by Aboriginals. But there has also been input by every group over a period of time. So that when I turn around and I say, "Look at modern Canadian foreign policy, at the whole idea of the honest broker, like it or not," and you say, "Well, where does that come from?" it can be acknowledged that it comes out of a very old tradition, which is probably Aboriginal, out of the seventeenth- and eighteenth-century experience of Europeans negotiating with Aboriginals. But its modern Canadian form comes largely in the nineteenth century from francophones not wanting to go down a straight empire route. So people like [Henri] Bourassa and Laurier were part of it. And then people like Defoe, and that whole movement in the Prairies for a change in attitude at the international level. You suddenly realize that it's actually an organic part of the country. It's not something we inherited.

I'll offer one example. Consider community freezers in Nunavut. In Nunavut, you move from camps where people come in with a caribou or fish and there are five families, so there is a tradition of dividing it up. That doesn't work when you're living in a town of four to twelve hundred, so all through Nunavut (and to some extent in Nunavut it's actually a policy), each municipality has a community freezer, and if you've got leftover meat or fish that you don't need, you put it in there. Then when the caribou are coming through, you go and hunt them as a community, and you put them in the community freezer. And when people need something, they go and get it. There's no administration, there's no signing of paper, there's no humiliation. No thanks are given for the contribution and no apology is required for taking.

That's a really interesting model when you compare it with food banks in the south, which are locked up in bureaucratic justification and apologies and thanks and managed rather heavy-handedly. How would the community freezer model compare with what we're doing in Montreal or Vancouver or Toronto? We have to do more of that kind of looking around the country for models and considering whether they can be carried somewhere else.

GEORGES ERASMUS: A very similar kind of model works among the Dene community. It might be a bit more administered because the local leadership would probably be wanting the meat to be distributed at certain times of the year, because once it starts to age, the taste changes and all the rest of it. So they actually cut it all up and go around and distribute it door to door.... It's virtually the same, but it has the Dene twist.

JOHN RALSTON SAUL: But it replaces the model in which we say, "You're poor, you need something and we're going to give you something." It removes the charity aspect. It simply says there is extra food available for whatever reason, which is very different from the classic charity model that we have in our cities in the south here.

ALAIN DUBUC: But are you saying that this is the Canadian value? Or instead does it show that you have very different values blending into a common identity, since people living in the south won't do that? It might help to know that there are some other models that work very differently.

JOHN RALSTON SAUL: I think it can be interpreted in two ways. Twenty-odd years ago, when people started setting up food banks, they thought they were doing it for a couple of months. They didn't realize it would slide into the normalization of the concept of class in our society. I think most Canadians are pretty uncomfortable with the idea of homeless shelters and food banks. I hear nobody saying it's a solution. So, in a sense, the value is shared. But because in the urban situations we're stuck in a model that is virtually a nineteenth-century class-based model, we can look at Nunavut and say, gosh, there's an interesting model. That's pretty much what happened in the early twentieth century. The farmers on the Prairies said, look, there's another way of dealing with women's votes, transfer payments, guaranteed incomes, pricing for grain. It seemed very foreign at first to other parts of the country, but within a five-year period, they were convinced, and they changed the national agenda. It's that kind of debate about the national agenda that is fed by the most original ideas coming from different parts of the country.

RUDYARD GRIFFITHS: Each of you in your speeches put forward new ideas and new models. For you, Alain, it was a vision of decentralization. Georges, you were encouraging a kind of nation-to-nation dialogue. Your Excellency, you were talking about the need to go back to some of our founding principles and values and begin a large-scale reform of these increasingly bureaucratic and complex organizations, which aren't necessarily delivering on those original values and principles.

There are some interesting tensions between those three kinds of models of reform or change. Alain, could you start?

ALAIN DUBUC: They're not models!

RUDYARD GRIFFITHS: Okay.

ALAIN DUBUC: One of the things we did in Canada was attempt to invent models and then to force them into place. They did not always fit with what the reality was, and I think we still have an idea of Canada that doesn't always fit. When I was talking about this on television. I didn't see it as a model that you can force on people but as a trend, as a way that people feel in defining themselves and recognizing similarities in a group. People are more comfortable identifying with smaller entities. If there's a model we can think about, it is Europe, even if they have some problems. We are seeing situations there in which some people suffer a lot from this loss of control of their destiny, but other people discover that being what they are — people from southern France or northern Italy and at the same time part of a great whole — is, in many ways, a very different experience. So you're French, you're sovereign French and you're European —

RUDYARD GRIFFITHS: And you're Mediterranean.

ALAIN DUBUC: — and so there's a much greater goal than just what you're urging the country to achieve. It's a kind of decentralization, where you're living in a smaller community but you adhere to something that is much bigger, with values that can bring you to evolve and to do something greater. It's not a model, but I think that is what we'll see in Canada.

RUDYARD GRIFFITHS: It's a concept.

ALAIN DUBUC: A concept based on what I see happening as a journalist. I see it in Quebec and I see it in other parts of the country.

JOHN RALSTON SAUL: It goes back to that idea of being comfortable. People in Canada are very comfortable with the idea that they are more than one thing at once. They might be holding back in the sense of participation on one level, because they're dissatisfied in various ways, as Georges points out. That happens in other areas as well. But they are comfortable with the idea that they can be several things at once. That is a form of decentralization. It's almost a psychic decentralization. This country has the flexibility inside it to readjust itself, and it does so constantly. It goes this way, it goes that way, you know. It does things that look impossible, and the day they are done they're no longer impossible. We have it in our minds that we don't have to be one thing.

At a time when, of the twenty-odd Western democracies, about eighteen of them are moving in the direction of the nineteenth-century Canadian model, it would be crazy for us to hold on desperately to an idea that we've never actually represented, which is an eighteenth-century monolithic model, just because we live next door to the one remaining country of all the democracies that still believes in that monolithic model. They are the exception to the rule. No one else actually believes in it. Europeans don't believe in it. Australians don't really believe in it. They are, in a way, like Canadians.

RUDYARD GRIFFITHS: Georges?

GEORGES ERASMUS: Well, it's really interesting to see our regional identities getting stronger. If you're from the Prairies, you know what you're going through now with the drought, and in fact people are leaving that part of Canada (apart from Alberta, of course). But I think the sense of community, if anything, is getting stronger out there. Obviously British

Columbia has the strength to grow, but you know the sense of identity and community there is quite strong.

I went through the interesting experience recently of having to move back to Yellowknife and experience the north again more closely than I had in some time. I noticed the changes that have happened there, who's involved. The kind of strict separation of community between Aboriginal and non-Aboriginal in different levels of the community in the north has really changed. The vision of Nunavut being created and the west staying part of the Northwest Territories has created a really interesting personality.

I do a lot of travelling across the country. My wife comes from Newfoundland, so for close to thirty years I've been going back and forth to Newfoundland, and the sense of community there is just immense. It's the same with the Atlantic provinces. For somebody going there, it's like a different world, never mind just a different country. So this concept that you are talking about of people identifying with the different regions, holding different values and so forth, is very true. You can experience it, and what's interesting is that there are a lot of universal values that still tie us all together. To me, this is probably going to be the interesting thing about where we're going to go as Canadians in the future, and it will probably, if anything, make us stronger. It might give us the kind of strength to build something like a collective character.

JOHN RALSTON SAUL: Or perhaps we're not able to admit that we've done it.

GEORGES ERASMUS: Maybe that's all we're talking about.

JOHN RALSTON SAUL: When I travel across the country, I find that people are very comfortable with values that are reasonably shared. But a lot of the public discourse, the official public discourse, which runs right through the entire country — in universities, politics, bureaucracy, journalism, historians — makes it very difficult to believe that there's anything there. But when you actually go out and talk to people … , when I go to Lac St-Jean, Quebec, whose do I find that discourse resembles most? Well, probably people in northern Ontario or Cape Breton or maybe Yellowknife.

Montreal's discourse, well, whose does it resemble most? Perhaps Vancouver's. In some ways Vancouver's resembles Montreal's most. And you could do this all across the country. The patterns are not the patterns that we're officially presented with on a regular basis.

I think everybody in this room has a sense of the positives and the negatives of the experience that we've all had in this country over the centuries. The public discourse doesn't take that into account. I use the word *linear* too much, but the public discourse is very linear. It doesn't really talk about the shape of the whole or the context or the circular nature.

I'm thrilled when I hear that pretty soon the workforce in Saskatchewan is going to be 50 percent Aboriginal. In a sense it brings us back to where we started the experiment. But it also means that there's going to be a completely new input of ideas coming out of Saskatchewan, and probably Manitoba, which is going to be about what happens when you have a southern territory with a major Aboriginal voice in it. Suddenly you have to come to terms with the whole history of the country, not just the year you happen to be living in.

ALAIN DUBUC: If it happens, you rediscover the virtues and differences.

JOHN RALSTON SAUL: Yes.

ALAIN DUBUC: And I think that Quebec is probably responsible for that, because differences there were seen as a tool to foster the separatist program. The situation in Quebec created a discourse in the rest of Canada in which this premise had to be denied because it would be seen as a menace to the structure. So you see the difference as a menace, as a weakness, while Quebec sees it as something manageable and rich in potential.

GEORGES ERASMUS: The same idea holds true for Aboriginal people.

JOHN RALSTON SAUL: The concept of complexity is the strength in the country. The nineteenth-century idea is that you can deny the complexity and so create a monolithic view.

ALAIN DUBUC: And the other thing is that the differences are useful to create the necessary tension you need in society. Because when we scratch the surface, there is much similarity and commonality.

RUDYARD GRIFFITHS: But people do see big differences in these small differences, at least in our public discourse. Our discourse is often very polarized, I would say, around Aboriginal issues. What forces are at play out there that are leading us away from an appreciation of the beauty of small differences to a kind of antagonism about small differences? Is it a democratic deficit?

JOHN RALSTON SAUL: Let's compare Canada with Europe. The big difference between us and Europe is that Europe has leapt ahead in continent-wide economic structures and political administration — that is, from the top down — but there's a vacuum when it comes to culture. People are inventing it. The southern French are inventing or reinventing a Mediterannean relationship with Barcelona and northern Italy. But actually little has been done on the broader cultural front, apart from one television channel and a few scholarships named after Erasmus. They still have an enormous way to go. Whereas we have a long experience of debating the cultural content and working with it.

I don't think one should be too worried about how noisy the debate is. This is a non-violent country that compensates, to some extent, for the absence of violence by debating in a very aggressive way. I believe that a lot of the adjectives and adverbs that we use take the place of the physical action you might find in countries where the language is more controlled. So when my European friends come here, they are horrified by our relatively violent public language. If that language were used where they come from, it would lead to action. And I explain that it is actually in place of the action. The reason that they talk so carefully is that they know that if they talk any louder, they might fall back into the pattern of killing millions of their fellow citizens, which they've done and continue to do. Think of Ireland, the Basques, Corsica and so on. It's a very different approach towards debate.

GEORGES ERASMUS: I think you're right. I had not thought about that point, but you're absolutely right. I think your point is very interesting because that's probably one way we're very different from Americans.

RUDYARD GRIFFITHS: So we're not as polite as we think we are?

JOHN RALSTON SAUL: Not in political debate. I'm always saying that we mustn't confuse social, middle-class politeness with the roughness of public debate. The roughness of public debate is very important in this country. It has to be rough to maintain that movement between the regions and the languages and the differences.

ALAIN DUBUC: You have different nations and you have tensions and you do have anger, and public discourse is a way of venting. This is why I am not afraid when I see tensions rise. It's part of the process. We have to let all these things out. You see it with the First Nations, too; they have to express their anger.

We have this myth about love. It's part of the way Canada seems to define its relationships among groups. We love each other and so when you see this tension growing people feel betrayed. But this is a naïve view of the nature of the relationship — it is not helpful to couch things in terms of love and hate.

RUDYARD GRIFFITHS: Is there a new way of listening to each other in this country? Is there something that Aboriginal people in particular are very good at, that could inform the way we listen to each other? Might it actually change the debate if we listened to each other in a different way?

GEORGES ERASMUS: Well, as I tried to suggest in the presentation I made, yes, it would obviously be better, because we would approach things from a different angle. We would try to look at how relations would be improved if we actually tried to regard the interests of everyone as equally important. But the reality is that we have structured the way things happen at the moment around government, and Aboriginal people and the rest of Canada are not involved. Unless Canadians really do get involved, I don't see things changing quickly.

There's a comment I wanted to make earlier about values and participation and so forth in the context of the discussion about NGOs. I wanted to tell you that, previously, Aboriginal people actually had more power in this country. In the past couple of decades, there was a huge coalition created across the country — church groups, labour organizations, university organizations, women's organizations and so forth — to lobby in support of very clear positions that average people have. It allowed a number of things to take place, and one was the postponement of the Mackenzie Valley pipeline. It took a lot of work to include Canadians, and we created organizations to work with southern communities. It made a big difference. Now that it's no longer there, you really can feel it. For instance, the funding for the Assembly of First Nations was cut in half, for whatever reason, just at the whim of the minister of Indian Affairs. Virtually nothing happens now. Whereas, while we were at the height of this coalition we created, that would not have happened.

JOHN RALSTON SAUL: I think the difficulty is that you can build coalitions outside, and they're very often essential. In fact, that's usually the way public policy reforms start. But historically what tends to happen, not just in Canada, is that in order for them to succeed in the long term, they become part of the inside debate, and they thereby take the argument of the coalition from the outside to the inside. And of course, that requires certain compromises, and in a way everybody is somewhat unhappy. But on the other hand, that does carry it into the mainstream. The argument was perhaps that maybe it couldn't happen at that stage because there were too many problems.

GEORGES ERASMUS: I don't know that that can always be the case, and I don't know if that is the conclusion, because there are only so many members, there are only two or three hundred members of the coalition, and what about the thirty million of us who are living in the country? That leaves us out in the cold.

JOHN RALSTON SAUL: Not really, because at some point there has to be a critical mass of people inside — on the committees, in the party meetings, in the meetings with the deputy ministers — who are part of that representation debate. There has to be a critical mass. It's almost a matter of how many times people sitting in the chamber or around the chamber actually voice certain opinions. Think, for an example, of the environmental question. You see that the absence of a critical mass of serious environmentalists inside is perhaps what has held it back, in spite of the popularity of the movement in most Western countries. The issue just hasn't been transferred over into representative politics.

GEORGES ERASMUS: I'm not disagreeing with that notion. You have to have strong representatives inside, otherwise you're always outside. But what I'm thinking is left out is that democracy has evolved to be an election every four years. You're a member of a party, perhaps, and you write letters to your MP, they have maybe two public meetings a year, and that's about it. If you're somebody who wants to take part, that's your only opportunity. We're still a long way from having the kind of society in which people can really participate.

We spend a lot of time in the north considering how we might create a society in the Dene area that actually reflects the values of the Dene. When we tried to do it, we found we needed more public participation. It wasn't possible for us just to create a society that redistributed our power among a few people and said, "Okay, you're the best among us, you govern," because it was so alien to the kind of values that we grew up with. We always maintained the right to participate, and we could exercise our right to have somebody to represent us, we could call them back if we didn't like what they were doing.

It's easier in a smaller society, and it gets more challenging with a bigger country and all the rest of it. But we're starting to get the means of communicating electronically and so forth, so it seems to me that we need to find ways to participate in this society a lot more than we do now.

ALAIN DUBUC: It works in small communities with small issues. People seem to participate in local politics, school boards, hospital boards because they are concerned. And it's the same in big cities. But when you're talking about NGOs and the mainstream, I think your question about how people don't listen to each other is truer with a majority. You usually don't listen to a minority. It's part of the normal life of a majority — not listening to and not taking into account the constraints that go with the dialogue. The only time you can engage the majority in dialogue is when you shout, when you make noise and annoy the majority and force it. And maybe it's the same way with some of the issues that are important within the majority. You have to force your issue or your cause to be taken into account. When it has no choice, the majority tends to listen, but the first reflex of the group is to deny problems or deny issues, because it takes them into account only when it is forced to. When you are first forced to look at the problem and then you see that you have a problem, this is when you change.

JOHN RALSTON SAUL: I think you're absolutely right about the question of participation, and I think probably all three of us agree that that is the biggest challenge. Reform has to end up in a place such as a parliament; otherwise, you're in a dangerous regime, which is direct democracy. We know that direct democracy can work in smaller communities and on smaller questions — not of smaller importance, but in numbers — because the people can actually either get together or almost get together. They can see how the participation plays out. The difficulty is that when we get to a million, seven million, thirty million, we really have to have a series of reverberations in order to get to what it is that we're going to do somewhere down the road.

We have done a lot throughout Western society, including Canada, over the past decade or so to discourage the idea that it would make a difference if you participated officially. People have become very discouraged about whether they can make a difference. All the assertions that there are great forces at work rolling over us makes people feel, "Well, why would I go to the local meeting if, after all, there are enormous economic forces at work that are taking my power away? Why should I bother?" I really think that the greatest labour that is there for those who believe in participation is to go out and relaunch, recreate, redefine the nature of participation for a citizen in a medium-sized democracy that has inside it all sorts of groups and minorities and languages and so on.

The other thing, at the centre of that argument, Alain, for me — and you'll say that this is a very anglophone argument, perhaps — is to really remind people, rather than convince, to remind people that the reality of Canada is that there is no majority and there never has been a majority. When one talks about the anglophones, for example, they were never one thing. They were always divided — either by their origins, going right back to the beginning with the Irish, the English, the Scots and the various other people who spoke English, or by religion or by region. They were never one group, and it was only very rarely in history, and usually at our worst moments, that somebody was able to assemble them as a majority, usually through anger, which is the worst kind of thing, and false love.

This has always been a country of minorities that at its best, or even at its medium-best, works most effectively as a country of minorities. And when you think about it that way, it makes you think about government differently, because suddenly you realize that the purpose of winning is to be able to deal with the multiplicity of minorities. Citizens are very comfortable with that idea. They're not really looking to be convinced that there is either a majority or a great majority.

Look at the relative success of developing stronger systems for French-immersion schooling, new rules for francophones outside of Quebec, and putting them in place both inside Quebec and outside of Quebec. That has a very interesting reverberation, I think, not simply for third languages such as Spanish or German or Chinese, but also for Aboriginal languages. Once you've shown, through systems such as those used for immersion French and for francophone minorities outside of Quebec, that French can work, then suddenly you think, well, there are some interesting examples here of why it should not be so difficult for Aboriginal languages to take not a defensive position but an offensive position.

So once you start entering into the spirit of a country of minorities, it doesn't lock anyone out. It actually makes it possible to imagine the other options that might otherwise seem very, very difficult. You know, when you say to people in Toronto or Montreal or Vancouver that there are fifty Aboriginal languages and we're losing them, they don't know what to say. But when you say to them, "Look at what we did with French in various places — and besides, these languages are part of the multiplicity of your culture — do you want to really lose them? Do you want to lose access to that?" then people say, "Well, we did it for this, we could do it for that."

RUDYARD GRIFFITHS: As a kind of a segue into a final phase for our discussion, could we have each one of you walk out on a proverbial plank and say where you see the potential for real reform and what shape that would take, if we were to re-imagine a new or democratic set of institutions and values, what would Canada be in fifty years?

ALAIN DUBUC: Fifty?

JOHN RALSTON SAUL: Not twenty-five, fifty? Where did this come from, this fifty?

RUDYARD GRIFFITHS: What would the country look like? Alain, in your case you talk about the North Americanization of Canada, and this may not actually be, for you, necessarily a bad thing, people thinking of themselves as part of a North American identity.

ALAIN DUBUC: I think that NAFTA — which was a business deal, a commercial deal, not a cultural deal at all — adds something wonderful. Mexico is now part of the picture, and it opened the minds of Canadians for the first time to a real foreign country. When you have trade negotiations with Americans, we are very integrated economies, so there was no real surprise in the fact that you could sell more into Maine or Iowa or Manitoba. But when you get Mexico in the picture, you begin to think in terms of another language, another culture and a society that is also a privileged one in some ways, and you have to think of your links to other parts of the world. We never did. Europeans did, and Americans did because they are a superpower.

RUDYARD GRIFFITHS: Are you saying there would be a fourth pillar in fifty years, adding Hispanic to English, French and Aboriginal ones?

ALAIN DUBUC: It's not the same. The language can be a tool to broaden our minds, but it will not become part of our culture. I do think, though, that we will begin to see the territory in a different way. Our conception of ourselves will not be the same either, so I think it will lead us to a much stronger identity than we have now. It will be the same for the Aboriginal peoples, because kids will go to the south and they will study and it will change their identity. It will be interesting.

But I'm not talking about reform, which was your question. It's about evolution. I'm not sure, because when we in Canada talk about reform, we talk about all kind of structures — how can we amend the definition? Maybe it will be very healthy for all of us for many decades not to think in those terms. And that is how you evolve. How you think differently is more important than what kind of reforms are occurring.

RUDYARD GRIFFITHS: So a discourse of values, not institutions.

ALAIN DUBUC: And cultures.

RUDYARD GRIFFITHS: Georges, how do you see the Canadian democracy in fifty years? What will it look like?

GEORGES ERASMUS: Well, we're probably going to be in a place where there's going to be a lot more land issues that have been resolved for Aboriginal people. The population is going to be interesting, because it's likely going to mean that in the Prairie provinces the workforce will be largely Aboriginal, and in the north also. So it's probably going to mean that the influence of Aboriginal culture is going to be stronger than it is now, because you're going to have a lot of people who have stopped being defensive and started to become creative. We will have been building for a long time, and you're going to have lots of places of strength in the Aboriginal community. You're probably going to see changes in medicine, for instance. Traditional Aboriginal practices in medicine will evolve in a way that brings together ideas that Western medicine has been working on for a long time and so forth.

You're going to see a very strong spiritual evolution. Christianity and its influence on Aboriginal people will not be as strong as it is at the moment because there's a rebirth happening in Aboriginal spirituality. You will probably still have a strong Christian influence, but what's going to be interesting is the rebirth — I didn't mention this in my speech, but it's quite immense, it's quite amazing what's happening in the Aboriginal spiritual beliefs.

So you probably will have strong Aboriginal languages, though you'll have lost a number. The ones that survive will be strong. And there will have been a pan-cultural process that has taken place because Aboriginals are looking everywhere for values, and it might not exactly be their own that they're looking for.

And then the other thing that's happening is that within a specific Aboriginal nation, there is growth happening there and knowledge emanating from it, so that we'll see both for a while. In the same way that Canadians share values, Aboriginal people are sharing as well. But within their own individual nations there has also been change happening. People are going back to, and understanding, what the original values were, and history and so forth.

I wouldn't be surprised if, at the national level, you have very strong Aboriginal politicians with more prominence than they now have, that are actually part of the centre.

RUDYARD GRIFFITHS: It would be part of the normalization of the Aboriginal role?

GEORGES ERASMUS: Yes, exactly.

RUDYARD GRIFFITHS: Finally, Your Excellency.

JOHN RALSTON SAUL: It seems to me that there are a couple of things, and one is that if you were to believe what is commonly said about the nation-state today, this discussion wouldn't need to take place. Theoretically, nation-states are becoming less and less powerful and less and less meaningful. My gut feeling is that what we're witnessing now — and I think it'll probably go on for at least a decade and perhaps more, because usually waves tend to be twenty or twenty-five years — what we're now witnessing is the return of nationalism in the broadest possible sense, simply because the movement for a quarter of a century has been to drive everything on the basis of economics and uncontrollable forces and that has produced fear, anger, alienation among a lot of people.

You can like it, you can dislike it, you can attribute it to many different things, but it's there, and you're starting to see the reactions everywhere. You're seeing a very frightening return of false populism throughout Western civilization, particularly in Europe, and a lot of things that ten years ago would have been considered impossible. Fascists in senior positions in government in Europe, once completely impossible, are now treated as normal in several places.

We were talking earlier about the body politic and how anger comes out. Well, you can see this wave of returning nationalism. Now, nationalism can be many different things. There are two implications to take out of this: one is that the nation-state isn't finished; probably the nation-state is not in the process of disappearing. And we are going to be faced, as everybody else is, with the question of what this means: is it going to result in what I call negative nationalism, or in positive nationalism or some variety of the two? Most of this conversation, I think, has been about the possibilities for positive nationalism.

You haven't heard a word here from the three of us touting the virtues of anything that would be traditionally called nineteenth-century nationalism, which I think we could call more or less negative. But that nineteenth-century nationalism is coming back all through the West.

And so part of the dialogue is trying to figure out how you give form to the positive aspects of it. What this country might look like in fifty years will be dependent to a great extent on whether we're able to give this value a shape. I think one of the key factors here is a particularity of Canada, which is this: no matter how much our population grows, it's going to be minute in comparison with our land; therefore, unlike Europe and the United States, and like Australia and a few other places, no matter how many people live in the cities, we have to maintain the tension between the place and the people. If we fall too much into the universalization of political science and economic theories about how a country works, we'll find ourselves attempting to apply theory systems and models that make sense in the United States and Europe but actually would be totally destructive for living here. And as the cities get bigger and bigger, they have a tendency to turn in on themselves — perfectly understandable. One can sympathize. You know, all three of us either are from or have lived in those cities. They have problems. But if they turn in on themselves, they turn their backs on the *place,* and that will simply accentuate the problems of both the country and the cities.

I think we have to come back to the question of participation that was raised earlier. If we can actually figure out ways for people to participate, that will take us down the road to positive nationalism, to the country working as an interesting experiment. And we have to keep thinking of it as an experiment. It will continue to be a place of minorities, and I think that the places from which the new ideas are going to come in the next fifteen to twenty years are probably not going to be Ontario and Quebec. I think they are going to come from Aboriginals, because of all the things that have been said: the critical mass is changing in the Prairie provinces, the north and so on. And besides, that's where there's the biggest change happening. Where the biggest change is happening is where the new ideas come from. We've got to open our minds to those ideas, and we have to stop being obsessed by what's still wrong in those communities and start saying, "Well, what's interesting that's happening?"

I think British Columbia is also going to have an enormous role to play. It's a bouillon of ideas at the moment. For example, to a great extent, environmentalism came out of British Columbia, and it may find a form that will change the face of the country. I hear arguments in Vancouver that, when you sit back and look at them from a distance, could be on the positive side, demonstrating the new impetus. And then I think, interestingly enough, that the Maritimes — which hasn't had a chance to bring a lot to the table for quite a while — did, in the nineteenth century, bring an enormous amount: the first democratic government, Joseph Howe, public education. I think the Maritimes are coming around an interesting corner, which is a combination of crisis and new ideas at the same time, and that the Maritimes may have something new to bring. I'm not quite sure what yet, but whenever I'm there, I sense something is happening, just underneath, coming up.

And then the final thing is — and this is almost administrative philosophy, what I talked about a bit in my speech three years ago — we have very successfully built up a whole range of public services in this country. Because we do it in an ad hoc manner, it becomes like an opaque mountain, and there's been a false debate about whether those services work. All that's wrong with most of them is that they are built up in the opaque stage, and that from time to time you have to clarify the purpose, the original and continuing purpose. It's a really, really boring process. It's law reform, really boring stuff, administrative reform, clarification. But if you don't actually deal with it, you can become a victim of the opaqueness. Then you end up thinking that the structure is more important than the intent. We have to get back to the intent of those policies and how they relate to the values that might be shared across the country.

ALAIN DUBUC: I have one more thing to say. The issue also has an impact on the way that we see this place and the necessity of this place. When we talk about the gap between public life and the needs of people, there's a certain relevance to government. The case then may be that some of the participation that we lost in the past twenty-five years can be recovered. I think it's possible because we will need to protect ourselves and to define ourselves, and globalization, of course. I totally agree with the concept of positive nationalism and in Canada we have an advantage that some European countries don't have: we have three kinds of nationalism in the same country. That can be dangerous, because they feed on each other, but the fact that we have three courses may provide a protection against the great danger of nationalism.

JOHN RALSTON SAUL: Related to that is the question, From where do we draw our new ideas? Some from inside Canada. But where do the ideas come from outside of Canada? I think it's problematic, and it's a return to the nineteenth-century colonial mind, to think that we have to draw from our closest neighbour. More and more we send our kids there for a brilliant education, but it's an education designed to run the most amazing and powerful empire in the history of the world. It isn't very helpful in training for people coming back to a country of thirty million who already think of themselves as minorities.

A concentrated effort needs to be made to create possibilities for Canadians to be educated abroad, post-graduate or whatever, but off the continent. I'm talking about thousands of kids going to Australia, going to Italy, going to Chile, going to Japan, going to Scandinavia. This has to happen if we're going to bring in ideas from outside, from places, from situations that resemble ours. I'm sure there are dozens and dozens of what I would call nuts-and-bolts things we could be doing that would change the pieces, the cards we can play with inside the country, the potential. Some of that's been happening among Aboriginals, Aboriginals moving around the world quite a bit, talking with other Aboriginal groups. New Zealand, for example, has had quite an impact, I think, in terms of shared ideas, no?

GEORGES ERASMUS: Yes, in fact one kind of globalization is definitely happening among Aboriginal people. It is the sharing of ideas and strengths, and it's something that I think is only beginning, because there's so much to share. And when you share when you're weak, you're actually strengthening again, and you build a community that you can provide for.

The Right Honourable Beverley McLachlin

~ **4TH ANNUAL LAFONTAINE-BALDWIN LECTURE**

Dalhousie Arts Centre
Halifax, Nova Scotia
Friday, March 7, 2003

Mesdames et Messieurs, distingués invités, j'ai l'immense honneur de prononcer devant vous ce soir le discours d'ouverture du quatrième symposium annuel LaFontaine-Baldwin. Dans ses activités d'écriture, le juge est le plus souvent encadré par des faits et des règles qui délimitent son propos, mais Son Excellence John Ralston Saul ainsi que l'Institut du Dominion m'offrent ici un terrain d'expression beaucoup moins balisé. Ceux qui m'ont précédée à cette tribune — un journaliste, un homme politique et un philosophe — ont partagé avec vous, sans contraintes, leurs valeurs les plus profondes. Je voudrais faire de même ce soir.

Ladies and gentlemen, distinguished guests, I have the great honour of delivering the opening speech of the fourth annual LaFontaine-Baldwin Symposium tonight. A judge is most often guided by facts and rules that delimit the extent of his or her remarks; however, His Excellency John Ralston Saul and the Dominion Institute are offering me here, a much less restricted forum for expression. Those who preceded me in this role — a journalist, a politician and a philosopher — shared with you, without constraint, their deepest values. I would like to do the same tonight.

One problem, more than any other, dominates human history — the problem of how we deal with those who are different than us. Human beings share a vast catalogue of commonalities. Our genetic differences are negligible; women and men are equally creative and capable; those we label as ill or old or disabled are no less virtuous, deserving or capable of contribution than others; and people from all cultures and societies share similar aspirations to be safe, to be loved and to feel fulfilled. In sum, the similarities that unite human beings by far overshadow their differences.

Why is it then that our differences dominate discourse on every level — political, legal, social and domestic? Our headlines tell the story. East against West in the Cold War. Serb against Croat in the Balkans. Hutus against Tutsis in Rwanda and Burundi. Barely do these crises subside than a new schism seizes the front pages — fundamentalist Islam versus the Western world. On the legal, social and domestic front we debate our differences with passion — the right of women to equal pay, the legitimacy of same-sex families, the place of religion in public life.

Tonight I propose to explore with you this issue. Why does difference dominate? How can we better manage difference? Canada, like other countries, has struggled with these questions. Sometimes we have answered them with exclusion and violence.

Yet even in our beginnings we find another response — the response of respect, inclusion, and accommodation. Accommodation, in this context, means more than grudging concessions. Accommodation, in the strong sense in which I wish to use it, means ending exclusion, encouraging and nourishing the identity of the Other, and celebrating the gifts of difference. It is this response that has come to characterize the modern Canada, shaping our thinking and our policy on women, First Nations people and the profusion of races and cultures that constitute Canada in the twenty-first century.

I will return to the Canadian experience. But first, let me take a few moments to explore the underlying dynamic of difference.

The Dynamic of Difference

Why, despite our manifest commonality, do our differences, real and perceived, tend to define our world and dominate our discourse and our conduct? Philosophers have long debated this phenomenon. Jean-Paul Sartre wrote of the Other as the concept by which we define ourselves. In his book on identity and language, *Oneself as Another,* Paul Ricoeur wrote of the "work of otherness at the heart of selfhood."[1] Michael Ignatieff has written movingly of "the stranger in our midst" in his book *The Needs of Strangers,* tracing the dialectic of difference and need in history and literature. Despite their varying contexts and perspectives, all agree on the essential role of difference in human experience.

An answer to the question of why we place so much emphasis on our differences lies in the inescapable human need to construct one's identity within a social context. For all the celebrated individualism of recent decades, human beings are social beings. "A person only becomes a person through other people," proclaims the African aphorism. To be human is to communicate, speak and relate to other human beings. As Charles Taylor reminds us, group living is a prerequisite to full human agency. Yet in this intercourse with others, we are confronted by difference; and in the face of this difference we are impelled to a sense of what distinguishes us as physically, historically and culturally unique. Indeed, we need this sense of identity to make sense of our worlds. Yet identity does not remain purely personal; identity itself becomes social. As we discover our distinguishing attributes — those elements in ourselves, our history and our culture that we value — we bind ourselves to others who share these attributes and values. In the process, each person becomes a constellation of group identities — race, ethnicity, language, gender, religion and a host of other affiliations.

Group identity is a good thing. It binds us to a horizon formed by a common history and shared memory in which we can orient ourselves and give meaning to our lives. It tells us who we are and reassures us that we are worthy. And it grounds our cultures — the aggregations of norms, achievements and institutions that are peculiar to a people. So long as group identity focuses on shared values, it is enriching and constructive.

But group identity can also be a bad thing. The obverse of commonality is difference. To say I am part of a group is also to say that I am *not* part of a *different* group. From here it is but a short step to seeing the different group as less worthy than the group to which we belong. What we see in the Other but not in ourselves may seem strange and abject. The celebration of the attributes of one group quickly slips into the denial of the attributes of others; the affirmation of one group's identity into the undermining of another group's identity. The positive "we are good" becomes the superlative "we are best," with its implication that those different from us are less worthy and less entitled to the full measure of human dignity and respect. Differences are magnified, even imagined, to serve the end of vaunting the merits of the dominant group. In its ultimate manifestation, this distortion of the group ethic results in the dehumanization of those perceived as different. They are no longer perceived as human beings, but as some lesser species whose rights may be denied with impunity.

The negative aspects of group identity tend to be self-reinforcing. Treating others as less worthy or able makes us feel stronger, more righteous, more powerful. We are doubly affirmed, first by our kinship with other members of our "superior" group, second by the presumed deficiencies of those outside the group. Treating those whom we perceive as different, or whom we do not understand, with dignity and respect is much more difficult.

The force of this dynamic of difference should not be denied but faced full on in its historical reality. As John Ralston Saul stated in his 2000 LaFontaine-Baldwin Lecture, "the past is not the past. It is the context. The past — memory — is one of the most powerful, practical tools available to a civilized democracy."[2] The history of human beings is the history of oppression based on real and imagined difference. The Athenians invented democracy, but women and slaves were not recognized as part of the polis. The Romans treated the peoples they conquered as slaves. Medieval Christians crusaded against the Infidel. Societies from Russia to India relegated ordinary folk to the subhuman rank of serf or "untouchable," denying them the most basic rights and opportunities. And in an atrocious distortion of group identity, the twentieth century witnessed the calculated dehumanization and destruction of Jews, gypsies and the mentally and physically disabled. We ignore this history at our peril.

This past is not our past; it is ever-present. Modern society condemns slavery, yet women and children still suffer its ravages. The world community decries discrimination, yet people are still treated as less worthy because of their race, ethnicity, gender, religion or disability. In Canada, we vaunt our multicultural society, yet racism, anti-Semitism and religious intolerance still lurk in our dark corners. The modern world holds out the promise of inclusion, but it delivers the reality of exclusion; the exclusion of refugees driven from their homes; the exclusion of women and minorities from mainstream institutions; even the more mundane exclusion of the schoolyard bully. We proclaim the right of every human being to life, yet so long as the memory of the events of September 11, 2001, remains we cannot deny that the stark goal of eliminating those seen as different dominates the agendas of many.

The imperative seems clear. President Woodrow Wilson's observation that "nothing ... is more likely to disturb the peace of the world than the treatment which might ... be meted out to minorities" is as true today as it was in 1920.[3] If we are not to perpetuate the tragedies of the past we must tame the dark side of difference. But how? Two solutions emerge.

The first solution looks at world history, deduces that human beings cannot be relied upon to treat those different from them with decency and dignity, and concludes that the only solution is to separate groups within autonomous nation-states. Michael

Ignatieff, in *The Needs of Strangers,* argues that ethnic groups "cannot depend on the uncertain and fitful protection of a world conscience defending them as examples of the universal abstraction Man,"[4] and therefore must be secured "their own place to be." The reorganization of Europe along ethnic lines and the creation of Israel reflect this thinking. And it is not without its virtues. As Georges Erasmus explained in his 2002 LaFontaine-Baldwin Lecture, self-rule confers a measure of respect and cultivates self-reliance and dignity. The sense of security gained from community self-determination is particularly important in cases where the countries of the world have been historically unable or unwilling to tend to the needs of given minority groups.

Yet for all of its attractions, the solution of finding an ethnic home for each of the peoples of the world does not offer the complete answer. First, in a world where most nation-states contain ethnic minorities and global movement of peoples is the norm, the ethnically defined nation-state is difficult to maintain. Second, even if one could achieve and maintain the ethnically defined nation-state, this would not prevent the confrontations between groups of states and ethnic blocks that dominate recent history. Third, the ethnic nation-state solution only addresses part of the problem — the political part. It leaves untouched and even threatens to conceal other forms of discrimination and exclusion within the nation-state because it says nothing about respect or the essential value of human beings. Finally, as Alain Dubuc warned in his 2001 LaFontaine-Baldwin Lecture, nationalism, "if it is exalted, ... can easily become a tool of exclusion rather than a window on the world."[5] We should not abandon the idea of the nation-state as one means of attending to the struggles of a pluralistic democracy; to quote John Ralston Saul in his 2000 Lecture, "[d]emocracy was and is entirely constructed inside the structure of the Western nation-state."[6] Yet if the goal is to address the negative potential of group identity, the nation-state solution simply cannot go the whole distance.

This brings us to the second way of addressing the negative aspects of difference — promoting mutual respect and accommodation within the nation-state. This approach rests on a single proposition — the intrinsic worth of every human being. In historical perspective, the idea is revolutionary. Throughout human history, the powerful and privileged have always treated those they view as different as less worthy. When historians look back on the last half of the twentieth century and the beginning of the twenty-first, they will describe the idea that all people are equally worthy as one of the seminal ideas of our time.

Yet the ethic of respect and accommodation possesses venerable roots. One hears its echo in the declarations of Western religion that all humans are created "in the image and likeness of God." The European Enlightenment contributed to the secular conception of fundamental human worth by celebrating the universality of reason, and Immanuel Kant urged that we treat humans as ends and never only as means. The Romantic movement furnished a robust notion of authenticity, premised on the idea that each person held a unique and intrinsically valuable potential that would be unlocked through genuine expression in life. These and other streams of thought converged and were filtered through the horrors of the first half of the twentieth century.

The result was a coalesced notion of the intrinsic worth of all humans and a palpable sense that social and political recognition of this idea was critical. John P. Humphrey, one of Canada's great contributors to the project of recognizing human rights, reflected this historical truth when he stated that, although human rights did not figure on the international stage prior in time, "[b]y 1945 ... the historical context had changed, and references to human rights run through the United Nations Charter like a golden thread."[7] We can now look back to the ultimate product of the work of Humphrey and others, the Universal Declaration of Human Rights, and find the clarion assertion that "recognition of the inherent dignity and of the equal and inalienable rights of all members of the human family is the foundation of freedom, justice and peace in the world."

Cette conception nouvelle de l'égalité fondamentale des êtres humains trouve son expression dans la langue du droit, par l'entremise de la reconnaissance des droits de la personne. L'égalité emporte avec elle le droit de chacun à la liberté. L'égalité n'existe que dans le respect de chaque personne. The new idea of the equal worth of every person finds expression in the legal language of rights — human rights. If all people are equal, it follows that all people are equally entitled to freedom, fair treatment and respect. The rights are easily stated. The more difficult problem is to move them off the sterile page and into the reality of people's lives.

Formal declarations of equality are not enough to remove discrimination and exclusion. Indeed, they may perpetuate them. Formal equality is the equality of "separate but equal." The group is hived off, labelled "different" and group members are told that they are equal with one important qualification — equal within their designated sphere. Cloaked by the facade of formal equality, group difference perpetuates denial. Examples are not hard to find. Formal equality allowed African Americans to live in forced segregation for decades. In the eyes of many, it still justifies treating women as different. You are equally worthy, these groups are told. It is just that you are different. Understanding and accommodating difference is essential to true equality. But when differences are manufactured, exaggerated or irrelevant, the result is to perpetuate inequality. True equality requires an honest appraisal of actual similarities and differences — an understanding of the context in which human devaluation occurs. To make equal worth a reality we need more than what Michael Ignatieff calls "rights talk." We need to look beyond the words to the reality, or context of the individual and group, to understand the Other in his or her full humanity. This requires an open and honest mind, a willingness to bridge the gap between groups with empathy. Only when we look at the member of a different group in this way are we able to give effect to the promise of equal worth and dignity.

Understood in this way, rights, like the nation-state, create a protected space for difference within society; a space within which communities of cultural belonging can form and flourish under the broad canopy of civil society. This applies to the traditional "individual" rights that enable individuals to form and maintain the groups that constitute civil society, to adapt these groups to changing circumstances, and to promote their views and interests to the wider population. Will Kymlicka states, "It is impossible to overstate the importance of freedom of association, religion, speech, mobility, and political organization for protecting group difference."[8] But a second kind of rights — group rights — are also important. These are rights that inhere in an individual not qua individual, but by reason of the groups to which he or she belongs, like protections for minority language and religion. "[W]ere it not for these group-differentiated rights, the members of minority cultures would not have the same ability to live and work in their own language and culture that the members of majority cultures take for granted."[9] Together, individual and group rights contribute to an ethic of respect for difference and meaningful inclusion of multiple Others in a diverse society.

Rights that acknowledge people as members of groups do not lead to a fragmented state. True, they are important to the communities they protect. But they also help us to reach across the borders between groups and to establish a civic community embracing sometimes profoundly different groups. The language of rights can serve as a common language of understanding. As Harvard Law Professor Martha Minow puts it, "[r]ights provide a language that depends upon and expresses human interconnection at the very moment when individuals ask others to recognize their separate interests."[10]

We must confront the dark side of human difference. We must recognize the price the marginalization of the Other in our midst exacts — a price we pay in the coin of war, suffering and unrealized human potential. We must provide refuges for our minorities — the physical refuge of the protective nation-state and the conceptual refuge of respect and accommodation embodied in the principle that all people, regardless of the group to which they are born or assigned, are equally worthy and equally deserving of respect. Only thus can we combat the discrimination and exclusion that have marred so much of human history.

The Canadian Experience

With this backdrop in mind, I now wish to turn to Canada's experience with the dynamic of difference and what it means for us as Canadians as we enter the twenty-first century. Formed as it was from powerful groups with different linguistic, religious and cultural attributes, Canada, from its earliest days, recognized the need to practise the habits of respect and tolerance and to enshrine them in the law through the language of rights. In order to form a nation, Canadians had to come to terms with difference by learning to respect other cultural and linguistic groups and by expressing a commitment to this respect through the provision of rights. Yet Canada was born in an era of ethno-nationalism, religious and linguistic intolerance, racism and gender inequality. These aspects of our past manifested as exclusionary, assimilationist and discriminatory practices at various periods of our country's life. We must also look at these dark points in our past and be humbled by their existence. So a close examination of Canada's past can disclose both a strong foundation in the ethic of tolerance and inclusion, as well as the dark side of group belonging in the form of intolerant treatment. I want to explore both of these aspects of our heritage in the hope of ultimately demonstrating that, as Canada has matured and grown as a nation, we have embraced and cultivated the first of these traditions in order to do a better job of confronting the second — we have learned to value and institutionalize the ethic of respect for difference as a means of combatting exclusionary thinking.

Canada is one of the few countries in the world that has from its beginnings dealt with the issue of minorities and subgroups by the two-pronged mechanism of the nation-state and respect and tolerance of minorities within the nation-state. Most of the world's countries grew up around and continue to adhere to the model of the ethnic nation-state, often in the face of diverse ethnic groups within their borders. European nations like Germany and France still cling — with increasing difficulty to be sure — to the ideal of ethnic nationalism.

Canada's history is quite different. Other countries are only now awakening to the critical issue of dealing with the Other in their midst. Canada, by contrast, was forced to come to terms with this reality from its very inception. The peace accords that ended the century-long wars between England and France in the late eighteenth century left England in possession of France's former colonies in America. Two of the most important — Quebec and the Maritimes — lay within the territory of the future Canada. People in these lands spoke a different language and adhered to a different religion than their new rulers. England dealt with these two distinctive colonies in different ways.

The first epitomized the ethnic-exclusionary approach to dealing with minorities. England required the Maritime Francophones, the Acadians, to conform, at least to the extent of swearing oaths of allegiance to the British Crown. The failure to conform, perceived or real, led to the deportation of the Acadians to what is now the United States and to far-flung points of Europe. Many eventually found their way back, but only after the separations and sufferings that inevitably follow such dispersion. The treatment of the Acadians remains a para-digmatic illustration of an exclusionary nation-state policy.

The Lower Canadian French population, on the other hand, was too large and too firmly implanted to be uprooted and disposed of in this way. England had little appetite for a conflict with its colonists in Quebec. And so, in the end, to truncate a long and complex story full of historical intricacies, it acceded to the demands of Governor Carleton (who camped three years in London insisting on his position) that the French-speaking people of Quebec be allowed to retain their language, religion and civil law tradition. Although motivated largely by pragmatic considerations, the product was a commitment to accommodation, embodied in the Quebec Act of 1774 — respect and tolerance, implemented through the mechanism of rights. Half a century later, discontent with colonial strictures led to democratic movements and rebellion in both Upper and Lower Canada. Lord Durham was sent out from England to find solutions. Lord Durham's Report of 1840 turned its back on Canada's history of accommodation and tolerance and recommended a return to an assimilationist policy that gave prime place to England and English traditions. But, under the leadership of LaFontaine and Baldwin, the colonials rejected Lord Durham's vision of the assimilated unitary nation-state. The former colonies of Upper and Lower Canada, Nova Scotia and New Brunswick that met in 1866 and 1867 to create the country of Canada had learned a critical lesson: the only way the new country could succeed was on the basis of a Constitution that guaranteed mutual respect and tolerance. And so Canada was born, not of nationalism, but of the pragmatic necessity to accept difference.

This beginning created the space in which the colonies, soon to be joined by the colonies of British Columbia and Vancouver Island, Prince Edward Island, the prairie territories, and later Newfoundland and Labrador, could come together and grow. Confederation and the constitutional guarantee of rights provided a mechanism through which the dialogue of accommodation could be pursued — a dialogue that is still being pursued today on all manner of subjects, from government provision of medical care and federal–provincial views on the environment to the rights of sexual minorities and Aboriginal land claims.

One of the most discussed issues regarding group difference in Canada has been the provision of guarantees for minority language rights. Language, as much as any other feature, marks the minority as different than the majority since language forms the basis of communication. Human beings seem instinctively to view those who do not speak their own language as outside their cultural group. It is thus no surprise that despite the reality that many countries are multilingual, a single common language continues to be seen by many as the essential glue without which a nation will fall apart. Thus the distinguished American historian Arthur Schlesinger, Jr., in *The Disuniting of America,* argues that it would be folly for the United States to permit Spanish to achieve any sort of official status. Schlesinger argues that "[i]nstitutionalized bilingualism shuts doors. It nourishes self-ghettoization, and ghettoization nourishes racial antagonism.... Using some language other than English dooms people to second-class citizenship in American society."[11]

In fact, however, the Canadian experience with bilingualism can be argued to support the opposite conclusion — that in states facing the reality of widely entrenched linguistic difference, recognition of the right to use minority languages furthers national unity. Canada's minority language and religion guarantees continue to serve their intended purpose — the purpose of providing security to minority citizens that the majority will respect their identities. Minority linguistic rights serve as a bulwark against fear of marginalization, allowing them to participate as equal citizens secure in the knowledge that they will not be excluded because of their linguistic identity. The economic cost of bilingual services is far outweighed by the benefits of inclusion. As Chief Justice Dickson stated for the Supreme Court of Canada in 1990, "any broad guarantee of language rights ... cannot be separated from a concern for the culture associated with the language. Language is more than a mere means of communication, it is part and parcel of the identity and culture of the people speaking it. It is the means by which individuals understand themselves and the world around them."[12] To draw linguistic interests into the protective embrace of the state is, therefore, a means of expressing society's commitment to the integrity of cultures and respect for the dignity of individuals.

En somme, la protection constitutionnelle des deux langues officielles au Canada souligne le rôle essentiel de la langue dans la conception que chacun se fait de son identité. Elle souligne en même temps le caractère primordial, pour notre société, de l'intégrité des cultures et du respect de la dignité de chaque personne qui s'exprime par des caractéristiques culturelles aussi riches que diversifiées.

Canada's foundation in the ethic of respect and tolerance provided space for citizens of two diverse cultures to work out their political, linguistic and religious differences in a climate of mutual accommodation. It did not, however, mean that the old exclusionary way of thinking did not persist. Sadly, against the backdrop of our remarkable history of accommodation and respect, Canada's first century was marred by the ethic of the assimilation and exclusion of peoples it slotted into special groups — its first inhabitants, the Aboriginal peoples; immigrants of so-called different races — that is, neither French nor English; and the 52 percent or so of the population who were women.

Our country's policy towards the ancestral inhabitants of Canada's lands, the Aboriginal peoples, has throughout its history veered between exclusion and assimilation on the one hand and respectful acceptance on the other. Prior to Confederation, Aboriginal groups were more often than not treated as autonomous nations. Indeed, the Huron and Mohawk nations played important opposing roles in the Franco-British wars on what was to become Canadian territory. But in the nineteenth century, as settlement progressed, exclusion, confinement and assimilation came to dominate Canadian policy. The results, most now agree, were at best a failure, at worst tragic. Only in recent decades have First Nations people begun to reclaim their group identity and their rightful place in our country.

The 1996 *Report of the Royal Commission on Aboriginal Peoples* laid bare for Canadians a history that can without exaggeration be characterized as institutionalized discrimination. The Royal Proclamation of 1763 recognized the entitlement of Aboriginal peoples to their lands and stipulated that these must not be taken from them unless they consented by agreement with the Crown. Translated into the Realpolitik of the nineteenth century, this meant the treaty system, whereby the Indians, as they were called, gave up right to their larger territories in return for a small parcel of reserved land — the reservation — and minor gifts. In British Columbia, treaties were not entered into; First Nations people were simply allotted parcels upon which to live.

The second-class status of Aboriginal peoples was clear. In 1857 Upper Canada passed the Act to Encourage the Gradual Civilization of the Indian Tribes in this Province, which provided for the enfranchisement of Indians of "good character," who would, thereafter, be declared to be "non-Indian." The theory was clear. Aboriginal peoples were regarded as "uncivilized savages." The only solution was to change them to "non-Indians," or in the words of Prime Minister John A. Macdonald to "do away with the tribal system, and assimilate the Indian people in all respects with the inhabitants of the Dominion." Following passage of the first Indian Act in 1876, Native cultural institutions and spiritual practices came under attack. On the West Coast, the potlatch ceremony was prohibited. On the plains, the police were called in to break up the sun dance, a ceremony thick with cultural significance for the Aboriginal peoples of the prairies.

In illogical locked step, assimilationist policies were paired with exclusionary practices in the pervasive reserve system. The very peoples the leaders were proclaiming should be assimilated found themselves virtual prisoners on their reservations with the Department of Indian Affairs' adoption of the pass system in 1885. The residential school system, established first in 1849 in Alderville, Ontario, and subsequently expanded, likewise combined exclusionary and assimilationist impulses, with the often tragic consequences that are only now coming fully to light. Policies were no better in the early part of the twentieth century. The assimilation-exclusion model persisted. On the exclusionary side, Canadian Aboriginals were not permitted to vote until the 1950s and '60s, unless they renounced their Aboriginal status. On the assimilation side, Duncan Campbell Scott, deputy superintendent of Indian Affairs, stated in 1920 that government policy was "to continue until there is not a single Indian in Canada that has not been absorbed into the body politic and there is no Indian question and no Indian department."

The simultaneous pursuit of exclusion and assimilation produced cultural displacement, marginalization and tragic loss of identity and self-esteem. The policy of exclusion cut Aboriginal peoples off from opportunities available to the rest of the country.

At the same time, the policy of assimilation undermined their identity as members of a group — their shared history, language and culture. The good aspects of the group dynamic — a solid identity rooted in one's history and culture — were weakened; the negative aspects — isolation, alienation and lack of opportunity — enhanced. Despite the often good intentions of well-meaning men, it is difficult to conceive in retrospect of a more problematic approach to the Other.

One can only grieve the loss to our country through the exclusion and undermining of Aboriginal cultures. I grew up in a small community in southwestern Alberta. A few miles from the school I attended lay the Reserve of the Peigan Peoples, a tribe of the Blackfoot Confederation, which had for centuries dominated the western plains area of what is now Canada and the northern United States. Apart from the people who came to work on the ranch from time to time I knew little of life on the reserve. My friends were my school friends. The Peigan children attended a reserve school. Equal maybe. But definitely separate.

In my final year of high school, two students from the reserve joined our class. They earned good grades, starred on the basketball team and excelled at art. Both wanted to go to university. One, in particular, wanted to become a lawyer. I remember George telling me of his dream; in those days such an elevated vocation for myself had not crossed my mind.

George, however, faced one formidable hurdle. In those days, admission to university in Alberta required a second language credit. The only languages accepted were French, Latin or German. George spoke two languages fluently: Blackfoot and English. However, despite excellent marks in all other subjects, he could not pass the departmental exam for French. So George did not head off to university with me in the fall. He went instead to Calgary to take special courses in French. I do not know much of George's end. But I do know that he never realized his dream of becoming a lawyer. Why? Because, returning to the theme I took up earlier, the ethic of formal equality was unable to comprehend his reality and accord him his full worth and dignity. The loss was not only his; it was ours.

Aboriginal peoples responded to the policy of assimilation-exclusion with "consistent resistance," as Georges Erasmus explained in his 2002 LaFontaine-Baldwin Lecture.[13] Recent years have witnessed community renaissance. Aboriginal peoples have begun a process of rediscovering their traditions and values, rebuilding communities, and exploring and sharing their cultures. Constitutional protections have been extended to the Aboriginal community, providing a legal safe-haven in which Aboriginal group interests can flourish. On the non-Aboriginal side, paternalism and exclusion are increasingly being replaced by respect and accommodation. To quote Georges Erasmus once more: "[g]aining recognition of Aboriginal rights in the courts and entrenchment in the Constitution have been critical to restoring Aboriginal peoples as active agents in directing our collective lives."[14]

Canada's history of minority exclusion and marginalization of those belonging to groups labelled "different" is not confined to the Aboriginal community. Chinese Canadians came to Canada to help build our railroads. Their task completed, they found themselves burdened with oppressive and discriminatory laws. Head taxes were imposed on entry. Impediments to the immigration of women were adopted. The lack of Chinese women in turn gave rise to irrational fears that Chinese men would prey on white women, and led to prohibitions on the employment of white women by Chinese men.

Black Canadians too felt the cold touch of exclusion and racism. Between 1782 and 1785 about 3,500 blacks, most former slaves who had fought for Britain in return for freedom, fled to what is now Nova Scotia and New Brunswick at the close of the American Revolution. Once in the Maritimes, they were cheated of land, forced to work on public projects like road building and denied equal status with whites. Disappointed, 1,190 men, women and children left Halifax on fifteen ships for Sierra Leone. Sixty-five died en route. In 1796, 600 Maroons — people with a long tradition of resistance to European rule — arrived in the Maritimes to face the same miserable conditions as the freed black Loyalists. They too left for Sierra Leone. In 1814–15, 3,000 or so American black refugees from the war of 1812 settled in the Maritimes, and in the 1920s hundreds of Caribbean immigrants, called "later arrivals," came to Cape Breton to work in the mines and steel mills. Quebec and Ontario saw similar migrations, and black colonies were established in the west of Canada. Black people came to Canada expecting respect and accommodation. They found little of either. Despite the abolition of slavery in 1833, black Canadians found themselves excluded from schools, churches, restaurants, hospitals and public transportation, and denied equal housing and employment opportunities.

The list of racial groups that have suffered exclusion and discrimination goes on and on. Ukrainian Canadians were interned in World War I. Japanese Canadians, as well as men of German and Italian origin, were sent to camps during World War II. Well into the twentieth century anti-Semitism forbade Jewish Canadians from holding property in designated areas. And in a dramatic expression of intolerance and lack of respect for the Other, who is labelled as different, legislation in the

mid-twentieth century permitted the eugenic policy of steriliz-
ing people deemed mentally deficient.

Perhaps the most far-reaching example of exclusionary
thinking is the history of our treatment of women. Women
make up 52 percent of the Canadian population. Yet for much
of Canadian history, women have been relegated to an inferior
status in society. Why? Again the familiar premise — women are
different. The obvious biological difference between men and
women was extrapolated to apply to all forms of feminine functioning. Women had smaller and less clever brains. Women were
congenitally weaker. Women functioned emotionally; only men
could think. From here it was but a short logical leap to
conclude that women should not be permitted to vote or practise medicine or law and should be barred from public office.
The effect of these illogical leaps into stereotype was to deny
women first-class status. Their identity as thinking, responsible
human beings was challenged, their humanity denied. People
perhaps, full persons, certainly not.

Women in Canada, as elsewhere in the Western world, began
to challenge these assumptions at the end of the nineteenth
century. They fought for legal rights and they won them. It took
a long time. Canadian women did not win the right to vote in
federal elections until 1920. And it was only in 1929, with the
now-famous "Persons Case," that the law recognized that
women were "persons" entitled to hold public office.

However, as with the struggle of Aboriginal peoples, legal
equality for women did not translate into actual equality. Old
ideas die hard. In the minds of many, women remained a fundamentally different kind of human being, with corresponding
fundamental limitations. Women were fit for domestic roles, fit
to serve as secretaries and nurses and other kinds of assistants.

They clearly were not, however, up to the big jobs. This exclusionist thinking was buttressed by ingrained attitudes that the primary place of women was in the home with the children. Women who wanted to serve in law, medicine or politics could attempt to do so, but they faced an uphill struggle against the prevailing attitudes of the day and seldom got to the top. The difficulties they faced led to statements like that of French journalist Francoise Giroud, "Women's problems will be solved when a mediocre woman holds a major job."[15]

It is now widely accepted that there is no justification for sweeping negative generalizations about the ability and temperament of women. It is accepted that women can and do play with equal effectiveness in all walks of life. And it is accepted — by many if not by all — that cooking and childcare is not an exclusively feminine gift; men too can enjoy and excel in these activities. Why then did we persist so long in our belief that women were fundamentally unsuited for anything but working in the home and assisting men in grander pursuits? The answer brings us back to the dynamic of difference. Instead of evaluating the differences between men and women honestly and with an open mind, people magnified those differences and extrapolated them into conclusions that bore no relation to the actual abilities of women and paid no respect to their right to choose their path in life. In a word, stereotype transmuted into popular, hence unassailable, wisdom. Myth supplanting reality shut women out.

Why did the myth of female inadequacy persist so long? Why indeed does it still exert a tenacious power over our deepest attitudes and actions? Why can we not simply acknowledge, as we increasingly do with ethnic minorities, that the biological differences between men and women should not limit their place in society? Why, in short, can we not, where women are concerned, move from an exclusionary mentality to an inclusionary mentality? The answers are complex. Social and religious institutions may buttress an exclusionary mentality, as may the very structures of our institutions.

For example, many Canadian offices and workplaces continue to be organized on the Edwardian model of a century past. The family breadwinner (presumptively Papa) is expected to be available for work and travel at any time. This is made possible because the family homemaker (presumptively Mama) devotes her exclusive efforts to the home and family. This model no longer fits the reality of Canadian families, where increasingly both parents must work outside the home to earn the necessary income and both parents are involved with domestic and child-rearing tasks. We are beginning to explore ways to bring our workplace organization into sync with the reality of our lives – daycare centres on the job site, childcare programs, flex-time and working from home are among the options being explored. So long as we organize our workplaces on Edwardian lines, women will find themselves at best stressed and at worst falling back into the default role of sole domestic caregiver, reinforcing the old attitudes.

Workplace organization is important. But so is workplace culture. "Why," I recently heard the senior partner of a national firm lament, "do so many women leave the firm after only a few years? They are among the brightest of our young recruits. We invest in them. We give them flex-time. Yet they leave in greater numbers than their male counterparts, usually for another job that entails just as much work. We know where they go but we don't know why."

It would be presumptuous of me to venture an answer to this honest and important query. Yet I am struck by a comment I recently heard: to be happy in a workplace one needs friends and at least one mentor. Here we encounter another aspect of finding a place for minorities in majoritarian institutions, be the minority a racial minority, a religious minority or a gender minority. The minority person may find the workplace culture hostile or, at the very least, less than comfortable. Sexual harassment was once common and tolerated in the workplace culture; it is now legally and socially taboo. Yet in more subtle ways, the minority employee may come to feel devalued. People need support. People need mentors. Members of workplace minorities may find less support and fewer mentors than members of the workplace majority. We should not be surprised if they then seek more supportive environments. The lesson is simple. Prohibition is not the only way to exclude. The Other in our midst may be excluded or marginalized in much more subtle ways.

If Canada has not won the war against the exclusion of women, we have fought the first important battles. We have rejected the exclusionary politics that once denied women access to the levers of influence, power and full societal participation. We lead other nations in the opportunities we open to women. We have more senior female judges, more female university professors, more practising physicians than many Western countries. Personally, I believe that in my own profession, the law, it is easier for a woman to succeed in Canada than almost anywhere else. Yet despite these achievements — and they are not inconsiderable — we still have terrain to take. Women's equality issues remain very much alive. Few women occupy the highest seats of political office and commerce. Statistics Canada tells us we have not achieved pay equity.[16] And violence against women is a persistent problem.

Canada's record on the treatment of Aboriginal peoples, racial minorities and women — not to mention gays and lesbians — teaches us that notwithstanding our nation's foundation in the ethic of tolerance and accommodation, we are not immune from the evils of exclusionary thinking. The natural inclination of the majority and the powerful to see the minority and less powerful as less worthy and less entitled to share in all aspects of the country's life has repeatedly surfaced on Canadian territory. We devalued Aboriginal peoples, ethnic minorities, disabled people and women, much as others elsewhere devalued the same groups. This must not be minimized. Yet from this complex and troubling history, we are slowly progressing towards a society where all people are fully valued, whatever their race, religion or gender. Since World War II and the international acknowledgement of the equal worth of all and the concomitant right to equal treatment, Canada has moved more quickly than many other countries to a more inclusionary, respectful model of society.

The law, while not the entire answer, has played a pivotal role in this progression. Canadian legislators reacted swiftly in the wake of World War II and the horrors of the Holocaust to protect minority rights. In 1944 Ontario passed the Racial Discrimination Act, which prohibited the publication or dissemination of materials that expressed racial or religious discrimination. In 1947, the Saskatchewan Bill of Rights Act began a revolution in legislation that sought to be broadly protective of rights and civil liberties. These legislative innovations dovetailed with the momentum building at the international level around the adoption of the Universal Declaration of Human Rights. In 1962, the first Ontario Human Rights Code proclaimed "the inherent dignity and the equal and inalienable rights of all members of the human family" ... "in accord with the Universal Declaration of Human Rights as proclaimed by the United Nations." Nova Scotia's Human Rights Act came in the next year, followed by Alberta, New Brunswick and Prince Edward Island. By 1973, all provinces had enacted human rights laws and in 1976 the federal government followed suit.

The adoption of the Charter of Rights and Freedoms in 1982 elevated the basic human rights, Aboriginal rights and equality to the status of supreme law, against which all government actions and legislation must be assessed. The Charter stands as Canada's ultimate expression of our commitment to freedom and human dignity. La Charte est l'expression ultime et profondément canadienne de la primauté accordée à la liberté et à la dignité humaine.

The Charter has had a monumental impact on Canadian law and, indeed, in what Kent Roach has called a "heavy export trade in the Charter,"[17] the law of other countries. Yet the Charter is more than a litigation tool or a lawyer's text. A glance at our newspapers shows the extent to which the Charter, and the values and principles it embodies, have been internalized by Canadians. Alain Dubuc has argued that the speed and readiness with which the rights enshrined in the Charter of Rights and Freedoms were taken up by Canadians was the product of an abiding national insecurity about our identity.[18] I prefer to think that the Charter manifests an ethic of respect and inclusion that has been part of Canada's fabric from its beginnings, and the way in which Canadians have embraced the Charter demonstrates its tremendous resonance with our country's identity. As I have tried to show, in Canada a unique political and cultural history is intertwined with a universalized ethic of respect and accommodation. The former constitutes our roots and shows us the path we have travelled as a nation. The second expands our sense of ourselves by including a commitment to respect for all kinds of difference in an unknowable future. Both are now immutable aspects of our country's identity, and both are reflected in the Charter.

In this way, the Charter, more than any other document, expresses the Canadian ethic, the country's sense of itself. The Charter also provides all of us, regardless of race, religion or gender, with a secure space in which to realize our aspirations. Finally, the language of the Charter provides a common vocabulary in which we can cast our various perspectives, giving all Canadians access to the public space in which some of our country's most difficult and contentious issues are debated. The Charter has not created consensus. But by expressing our most fundamental values — above all the respect we hold for others, regardless of their differences — it has strengthened us and given each of us a place to stand. And by giving us the common vocabulary of rights it has provided a forum for understanding one another's circumstances and working out the accommodations so essential in a diverse, multicultural society.

The Charter protects difference. But, independent of any particularized rights, respect for minorities has become an inseverable component of our constitutional fabric. On August 20, 1998, the Supreme Court of Canada rendered its judgment in the *Reference re: the Secession of Quebec*.[19] Noting our long tradition of protecting minority rights, the Court recognized the protection of minorities, along with federalism, democracy, constitutionalism and the rule of law, as one of the foundational principles subtending our constitutional architecture.

Canada, as a nation grounded in difference and respect, has erected an impressive legal structure to protect difference. But this structure is not merely law. This is no alien, imposed legal order. It is a structure that expresses our history of respecting minorities and our ever-strengthening commitment to the policies of inclusion and accommodation and to the belief in the fundamental dignity and worth of each human being. Inclusion and equality cannot be achieved by mere rights. But when the rights reflect a nation's values and are accepted as a means of brokering our differences and finding accommodation, they take on profound importance. And when we add to the mix attitudes of tolerance, respect and generosity — attitudes that Canadians possess in good measure — the prospects become bright for the inclusive society of which we dream. Michael Ignatieff writes in *The Needs of Strangers* that "Love ... is perhaps the most desperate and insistent of all human needs. Yet we cannot force someone to love us. We cannot claim love as a human right."[20]

My hope is this. If we cannot claim love, we must strive for respect and accommodation. And as national ambitions go, that's not bad.

Notes

1. P. Ricoeur, *Oneself as Another,* trans. K. Blamey (Chicago: University of Chicago Press, 1992), 318.

2. J. R. Saul, A. Dubuc, G. Erasmus, *The LaFontaine-Baldwin Lectures: A Dialogue on Democracy in Canada,* vol. 1, ed. R. Griffiths (Toronto: Penguin, 2002), 3.

3. Plenary Session. 31 May 1920: HWV Temperley, *A History of the Peace Conference of Paris,* vol. 5 (London/New York: Oxford University Press, 1969).

4. M. Ignatieff, *The Needs of Strangers* (London: Penguin, 1984), 53.

5. *LaFontaine-Baldwin Lectures,* 59.

6. *Ibid.,* 24.

7. J. T. P. Humphrey, *Human Rights & The United Nations: A Great Adventure* (Dobbs Ferry, N.Y.: Transnational Publishers, 1984), 12.

8. W. Kymlicka, *Multicultural Citizenship* (Oxford: Oxford University Press, 1995), 26.

9. *Ibid.,* 126.

10. M. Minow, *Making All the Difference* (Ithaca and London: Cornell University Press, 1990), 296.

11. A. Schlesinger, *The Disuniting of America: Reflections on a Multicultural Society* (New York and London: W. W. Norton & Co., 1998), 113.

12. *Mahe v. Alberta,* [1990] 1 S.C.R. 342, para. 32.

13. *LaFontaine-Baldwin Lectures,* 118.

14. *Ibid.,* 104–105.

15. As quoted in Lysiane Gagnon's column in the *Globe and Mail,* Jan. 27, 2003, A15.

16. Statistics Canada, *Average Earnings by Sex and Work Pattern,* based on CANSIM II, table 202-0102.

17. K. Roach, *The Supreme Court on Trial: Judicial Activism or Democratic Dialogue* (Toronto: Irwin Law, 2001), 60.

18. *LaFontaine-Baldwin Lectures,* 72.

19. [1998] 2 S.C.R. 217.

20. *The Needs of Strangers,* 18–19.

David Malouf

∾ 5TH ANNUAL LAFONTAINE-BALDWIN LECTURE

Convocation Hall, University of Toronto
Toronto, Ontario
Friday, March 12, 2004

We sometimes assume that only in new societies, in settler nations like Canada and Australia, is identity a matter of question and doubt. In fact these questions also arise in older places. I'm thinking of the united Germany and how, on a daily basis, whenever rights are under consideration or laws made, or an historic monument is to be restored or a bit of waste ground built on, there is always the need to take account of recent history; not in order to rewrite it — quite the contrary — but to see that the new thing continues some aspects of the past and makes a break with others.

Nations that have suffered defeat and occupation or have condoned or been the victim of tyranny, or of civil war or violent social division — England after 1649, the United States after its civil war, more recently Chile, South Africa,

Lebanon, Cambodia, ex-Yugoslavia and many more — have in the re-establishment of civil order within a unified and bonded nation to face bitter questions about crimes committed and rights violated before they can be reconstituted as ventures with a foreseeable future.

Australia, too, I might just say, has a problem, still unresolved, with history and the need for reconciliation. Unlike Canada, we did not recognize prior occupation of the continent by indigenous people. Until very recently, we considered it, before we arrived, to have been *terra nullius,* no man's land. We signed no treaties with native peoples, and till 1967, when a referendum settled the question, did not count them in the federated nation. They were, in 1901 when we drew up our Constitution, no more than an unhappy remnant. Their only chance at a life within the nation was to assimilate or get lost.

But with this admittedly shameful exception, our nation, like yours, does not have a past of violent disruption, of civil war or revolution or tyranny to deal with. Questions of identity in new countries such as ours are about who we are and what we are for, have to do with beginnings and ends. With the kind of worlds we have made through the give-and-take of daily intercourse, but even more through inventiveness and imagination, that might offer us a security and range of opportunities that are not common elsewhere.

Of course the particular conditions out of which the two places grew were unique, as they always are. What we now call Canada and Australia had different beginnings.

You began as a series of isolated settlements and trading posts in a vast wilderness that became, over centuries and by agreement, a tripartite nation, British, French, native.

We began nearly three hundred years later, as a purely British venture and a planned one: a product of the English and Scottish Enlightenment.

Despite these large differences, we are at this point remarkably alike: federations that share the same goals and values, the same responsibilities one to another as members of a society devoted to the public good. We have two of the oldest and most stable government systems in the world and legal systems so close that decisions in your courts are frequently referred to as precedents in ours. We also have similar views about where we stand in the world: our responsibility as middle-sized but rich nations towards those out there in a complex world (and in our case they are close neighbours) who might need our aid or protection.

So then, what sort of nations and countries — since nation and country are not quite the same? What values and how did we establish them? To what extent have they been achieved? And how, in the world as it now is, are we to extend and preserve them?

We are places, I would want to say first, whose great work is to comprehend, which really means imagine, the land we occupy. To take it in. First as a land mass — much of which, desert in our case, ice in yours, is very nearly blank, though not in the minds of native people — then to hold it in our mind as a place fully occupied and inhabited: so fully that all the events and accidents of our experience in it, all the acts of conscience, somehow persist as accumulated lived life to enrich and layer the present and give it depth.

I am speaking now of our kind of history. Which is not one of great men or heroes — we are very little concerned with those — but of experience and the density of living: of work done, houses and cities built, many small lives lived that made their own small mark. A country imagined but also held in the memory, remembered, and in this way carried forward as a present reality to be dealt with and drawn on, but also loved.

This is the work of a particular kind of country. One created by settlers who have first to discover it on the globe and then in their consciousness: one, in our case, and in yours, that was already possessed and fully imagined and inhabited before we came to it, so that as well as the form we have conceived for it there exists an older and parallel one that is haunting, mysterious, and perhaps finally unknowable to us, but it is also an assurance, if we needed one, that the work can be done.

Australians took a long time to recognize this as the real work of settlement. Till our country, in 1942, was in imminent danger of being taken from us. On February 24, 1942, 13,000 of our men, two whole divisions, went into captivity at Singapore; four days later Darwin was bombed and over 300 killed; the Japanese were in East Timor. We saw then, and for the first time most of us, what it might be that we had taken custody of, and had to ask ourselves what we had made of it that was worth the preserving; whether in fact it was really ours. It was the moment, perhaps, when we learned to see at last how native peoples possessed it and what we might have to learn from their experience: how to possess the place inwardly, and so subtly, so much as part of our life-blood that even if the land was stolen from us we could not be dispossessed.

So then, beginnings.

Precisely where the venture we call Canada began must be almost impossible to determine; like deciding at what point all the sources and little tributary streams of a river come together to make a single course that can be identified and named.

One significant moment, no doubt, was when the two men who give their names to this lecture series, LaFontaine and Baldwin, bringing with them their people, their language groups and the experience they represented, made common cause to win responsible government.

Equally decisive was the reaction of the LaFontaine-Baldwin administration to the burning of Parliament in 1848.

The very year, 1848, offers a dozen examples across Europe of how violent challenge to authority might have been met. Your authorities chose to go against conventional wisdom and practice, and by a bold act of imagination and faith in the people lay down a new law. In this place violence will not be met with violence because authority here is to be founded on something other than force. Let's see how *that* works, since we know already that the other does not. What was being established was the temper of a new world — one different not only from Europe but also, as would soon be demonstrated, from the United States.

The beginning in our case is easier to establish. It has an hour and a day: the evening of January 26, 1788, when the male convicts of the First Fleet and their marine guards came ashore — the women would remain at Botany Bay for another ten days or so — the Union Jack was raised and the king's health drunk. The argument in our case is what it was exactly that was being founded: a penal colony under naval administration and within the control of the East India Company to take the over-flow of English jails, or — as seems more likely considering the huge cost, at £65 per convict — a naval station to supply a new and faster route to India and to be a watchful presence in the South Pacific against the French.

Either way, the notion was to create a transported version of the motherland where men and women who had been delinquent in one hemisphere, and in their first life, would be remade as good citizens in another. An Enlightenment experiment in the reformation of criminals and the creation, on the dark side of the planet, of a new Britain where the darkness would be illuminated by British know-how, Protestant order and decency, and the law.

A risky venture, but one that worked — though only just. The conditions were harsher than expected, the climate and seedtimes were unpredictable, the natives did not practise agriculture and could not help. What was essential to the experiment was adaptability, resourcefulness, and since old rules, old habits and traditions were useless in the place, a devotion to the principle of "whatever works" — all qualities that were highly developed in the practised criminals who made up the majority of the new inhabitants, but were also qualities of the peculiar Anglo-Saxon "turn of mind."

It was the particularities of the place itself that determined what must be done — and in response to them, and in interaction with the contingencies they threw up, this very particular society, which quite soon in no way resembled the one it was supposed to mirror "at home."

This was a complex and diverse society, as all societies are, divided by tensions that were local and particular. Think of your own world here in the first half of the nineteenth century, out of which some kind of non-violent civil society had to emerge from the conflicting views of reformists like Baldwin and LaFontaine, the Chateau Clique, merchants, railway barons, loyalist Orange Lodges that were anti-American, anti-Catholic, anti-French.

The tensions in Australia were of their own kind. Between the native-born and the immigrants; between free settlers and emancipists, that is, convicts who had completed their sentence and now wanted the right to serve on juries and stand for elected office; Catholics, largely Irish, and Protestants, who were also divided between Anglicans and non-Conformists; and between big landowners, "squatters," on the one hand, who saw themselves as an emergent aristocracy, and smallholders and city workers on the other. Because even convicts had from the start been granted Crown land — fifty acres to a man on a completion of his sentence, thirty to his wife and to each child — land in Australia represented currency and the surest way to respectability and status.

As a child of Empire, my vision of Canada — "Our Lady of the Snows," Kipling called it in one of his imperial odes — derived from the tales of the rugged outdoors I read in *Boys Own Annuals* and from an advertisement on Australian radio. Out of a roaring blizzard came a voice intoning: "for coughs and colds, do as the Mounties do in the frozen wastes of the Canadian North. Take Buckley's Canadiol Mixture."

But myths and stereotypes apart, our experience of space, our need to accept that there are areas within the worlds we inhabit that must remain forever beyond knowledge or control, has profoundly affected our view of nature and our place in it. In ways, too, that are essentially un-European.

For us nature does not offer that comfortable reassurance of human centrality and power that in Europe comes, quite literally, with the territory. At worst hostile, at best indifferent, it does not offer us moral consolation or make itself available as a mirror of human existence: there are no sermons in these stones. What it does is raise questions about what necessary place we humans might have in a world that exists quite well on its own and that has, in the end, no need of us. Now there's a challenge! To recognize and accept this and live, not too uneasily, with the sense of limitation it imposes. To accept, too, that the presence among us of native peoples with a very different view of man's responsibility towards the earth — his right to use and change and shape it — tends to limit any belief we might have that our own Western way of dealing with things is the only way that is right and human.

And the experience of space shaped us in another way. It existed in the mind of even the most confined city-dweller as the one commodity in a poor country — which is what we were, both of us, till fifty years ago — that was always in large supply. Space as *room*. Room to breathe, room to move, and a belief that we could afford to be generous in making room for others. It didn't always work, and we need to recall the lapses of this spirit of openness in us: in our case the hostility in the nineteenth century to the Chinese, and in the 1920s to southern Europeans; our treatment of aliens, even if they were natural-ized, in both wars; and of asylum-seekers now. But for most of our history a sense of physical space, and its reflection in us as psychological space, have made us open to possibility both in the society at large and in ourselves and have encouraged us to be open as well to others.

We are such rich places now that it takes a small exercise of retrieval to recall that for most of our history it was struggle and heartbreak that shaped what we have of a national character and our notions of what a good and just society might look like.

It was hardship, isolation in the bush, grinding poverty in city slums, that created the hard-bitten stoicism of Australians, their skepticism towards every sort of utopian promise, their frugality, their dry humour, their tendency to cut down tall poppies and resent outsiders — overseas bankers, immigrants who might become a pool of cheap labour, theorists, ideologues, the bearers of modernism, and, as the other side of all this, that spirit of mutual regard and help we call mateship.

The idea of the battler dies hard in Australia, even among conservatives. There is no shame for us in needing a helping hand — in the bush you could not do without it, and it has always been accepted in Australia that if we are to get by and live decently it is the business of government to readjust, so far as it is possible, the inequalities that come from bad luck, lack of opportunity or the many other factors in a complex world that might bring a person down. There has never existed in Australia that fundamental distrust of government and resentment of government interference that was there in America from the beginning. Jefferson's proposition that the tree of liberty is watered with blood, like the American right to bear arms, has no place in our world. We see government as an arm of our will. We give governments money so that the poor, the sick, the old, the disabled, the unemployed, can live in a way that will not, as neighbours, shame us.

The one word that sums up what Australians demand of society, and of one another, is *fairness,* a good plain word that grounds its meaning in the contingencies of daily living. It is our version of liberty, equality, fraternity and it includes everything that is intended by those grand abstractions and something more: the idea of natural justice, for instance. It's about as far as most Australians would want to go in the enunciation of a principle.

We have no equivalent of your Charter of Rights and Freedoms, and the attempt on the centenary of Federation, in 2001, to produce a new Preamble to our Constitution resulted in little more than pious generalizations. There is some agitation for a Bill of Rights, largely as a way of enshrining rights for

indigenous people, but it shows small sign of being implemented. Perhaps it is our preference for precedent over principle
that makes us cling hard to experience rather than written codes
as our guide to choice.

The appeal to fairness, for example — "it's not fair!" is one of
the earliest formulations a small child discovers to express a
recognition that life is a game that ought to have rules — immediately sets a question that might be difficult to argue in purely
abstract terms, in a context where we are forced to recognize the
subject of the question as another like ourselves; as if *we* stood
where he or she stands and the subject was ourself. It is on these
grounds that such questions were resolved — and most of them,
by world standards, very early — as who in the new worlds we
were creating should get the vote. All men, including those who
did not own property? Catholics? Jews? All women? Aborigines?
The real question was, what argument for *unfairness* would have
to be mounted to make exclusion possible?

I have been speaking here — directly about Australia by
reflection about Canada — of the kind of forces — responses and
adaptations to the particularity of place, imaginative leaps into
the realm of social possibility — that have produced the very
complex and original, but stable and secure societies we now
enjoy.

There are continuities here, since history is not "the past" but
all that experience that has got us where we are, and which determines what we have as a guide now to dealing with the present.

The ease with which Australia has, in just a few years, moved
on from being a basically British society to one that is complexly
multi-ethnic is only one more example of that adaptability and
openness to change, to transformation, that was applied in the
early days of the colony. And the same is true for an even larger

shift we have made; from a nation that lived, as we used to say, off the sheep's back to one whose economy now is based on services — tourism and the hospitality industries, education, IT — or on such high-tech products as fibre optics and advanced medical techniques. In 2000 we earned more from education than from wool. This is not just an economic shift. It has also, especially for Australian men, been a psychological one that asks them to redefine the way they see themselves and their maleness. All these adaptations and transformations have had to be made, as they always are, on the run.

Societies are improvisatory affairs, made from moment to moment and by many hands: they are of their very nature open and unfinished. The question is whether that formal thing we call a nation can be open and improvisatory in the same way. It's a question, it seems to me, that Australia and Canada have been exploring for most of their lives as nations, and given our very different conditions and history, in something like the same way.

When, after two decades of rather acrimonious argument, the Australian colonies decided, in 1901, to federate, they had a long history of separate existence and had their own very different styles of life. They had been founded at different times and by groups with very different notions of what they meant to be; had their own armies and navies, their own trade agreements with Britain and with the Colonial Office and the Privy Council, their own police forces (we have never had a national police force like your Mounties), their own systems of education, and their rail-systems had different gauges. That Australia was a single land mass did not necessarily mean, at that point, that the continent had a manifest destiny as a single nation. The first rather cautious exploration of a single Australian identity — rather appropriately we might think — came with the unified cricket and rugby teams we sent to Britain in the 1870s. In the first draft of the Federation, places were reserved for New Zealand and Fiji.

Federation was a choice — the people's choice in a referendum — but a reluctant one. As the world's fourth federation we looked to the U.S. and to Canada as models and took something from each. Unlike Canada, we named the limited powers that would go to the Commonwealth — trade and external affairs — and the states retained the rest. The states, more than a hundred years later, remain separate and strong; wary of one another and even more wary of Canberra. Especially of Canberra's tendency to argue, in its own interest, that our present three-tiered form of government is wasteful and inefficient, the push by Canberra policy-makers for a formalizing Bill of Rights, and the signing by Canberra of UN declarations that impose laws on us that have not been put to the people's representatives or to its courts.

It takes a particular temper in a people, a particular feeling for order, and flexibility or looseness, to make a successful federation; a willingness to forego the centring of authority in a single place to a recognition that there may, without the whole enterprise flying apart, be room for several centres in dialogue but also in argument with one another.

To be comfortable with federation demands a certain state of mind and, more importantly, encourages it. We learn to enjoy diversity and seek it out, to find interest in difference, to relish the curiosity it rouses in us, the surprise it brings, the originality it tempts us to in ourselves, the new forms we learn to create through mixing — or "fusion" as Australians call it in the case of food. We were too mixed from the beginning to be tempted by notions of purity, though Australians did for a time, in the great heyday of nationalism in the late nineteenth century, have their own dream of a manifest destiny. It was that if Australia could be kept white, and remain predominantly Protestant, it might become the survival ground, when Britain itself failed, of British virtues and of the British way of life. What is surprising now is not how strong the dream was, or how long it lasted, but how quickly it has faded and been forgotten.

Australia is not much held together by national sentiment. We still think of ourselves, except in sport or war, as Queenslanders, South Australians, Sydneysiders. We seldom fly the flag or sing the anthem, which was only decided on, by vote, in the 1980s, and most of us, after the first two lines, do not know the words. Those who do tend to scoff at them. It's the kind of nation most Australians feel comfortable in. Regionally diverse, highly decentralized, though Canberra in recent decades has enormously increased its power in national affairs (the federal government has the exclusive right, for example, to raise taxes), it is loose, casual, off-handedly humorous towards the things that usually constitute nationhood, but it is also in the event remarkably cohesive and has survived without disruption for more than a century. Australians are happy with this fragmentary and provisional embodiment of what we might be, a nation "in the making." We get our clearest glimpses of it not on official occasions but when we find ourselves almost by accident in situations where we look about, see who is present and say, "Ah, so that's who we are!"

Election days seem to me to be such occasions. Given that voting is compulsory and always takes place on a Saturday, the whole population is abroad: the day has the mood of a national holiday.

Otherwise such occasions can be unpredictable. Like the procession of the Olympic torch through Sydney, for example, when two million people turned up to an impromptu festival at which the real spectacle, in the end, was themselves.

In fact we do have a national day, Australia Day, January 26, which commemorates the landing at Sydney Cove. There are citizenship ceremonies, multicultural dancing, fireworks; celebrity ambassadors — a curious idea — are sent out to tell their fellow Australians what the day means to them. It has never caught on. Imposed from above, it celebrates an idea of nation that has never really taken, and there are many of us who feel uncomfortable with a day of national unity that some among us — Aborigines — see as a commemoration of invasion and dispossession.

What *has* emerged — slowly over recent decades and strongly in the last — is a nationwide response to Anzac Day, the commemoration of the landing and massacre of Australian and New Zealand forces at Gallipoli, Turkey, on April 25, 1915. As it has passed out of the exclusive guardianship of veterans' associations, this day has become a genuinely popular occasion, reclaimed and re-shaped by Australians at large as an occasion of many meanings: a solemn day for meditating on war, on service, on loss, on the tragic in life. That it keeps developing new significances, especially among the young, is the clearest indication that it is a living thing and will survive. A national day we have made out of bitter experience and a need for the consolations of ceremony, it speaks for another form of nation than the official one: a nation based on shared experience and dispersed in varied, complex and even contradictory feelings, but no less bonding for that.

One other factor that increasingly, I think, determines the way we see ourselves and the world.

Nothing defines a people more clearly than what they fear. Anxiety in your case springs from proximity — I'm sure I don't have to be more specific; ours from distance.

Our remoteness, down there in the south, might have made us independent. London for most of the nineteenth century was three months away; we were on our own, and far, as you were not, from interference. Instead we felt anxious and unprotected. Afraid that we might fall out of the world's consciousness, slip off the edge and be lost. What if history happened without us? Hence our eagerness to get in on all those *wars:* in the Sudan in the 1890s, the Boer War, World War I, in which we lost 62,000 men out of a population of four million. More insidiously, afraid of losing our whiteness, and going native or creole. Or of losing the attention of what was, after all, the major power of the day, of no longer being included in its wealth and influence or having the protection of its navy.

Canada has always, it seems to me, taken a bolder and more independent stance than we have. Towards the U.S. certainly but also towards Britain: over independence in the 1920s and '30s, over Suez, most recently over Iraq. We actually refused the independence you worked so hard for when it was offered us in the Statute of Westminster. We found it "unnecessary."

Perhaps distance has led us to believe that we can play with the big boys without falling too deeply into their hands. Placed where you are, you have never had that luxury. On the other hand you have never come close, as we did in 1942, to invasion, and you do not live, as we do now, in an "arc of instability" — of potentially failed states.

You will have gathered by now that I do not have much to say about the nuts and bolts of politics, or of economics either. That is not because I don't think these things matter. They do. But what gives them their life and force as practice, and makes the practice assume this shape rather than another, are experiences, apprehensions, needs that work far below the level of event, and far below that realm, too, of argument and decision that brings one event rather than another into being and determines the particular shape and style of institutions. It is what belongs to this *lower* layer of a people's life that I want to point to. The experience that embodies a people's interaction with the land they find themselves in — its spaces, its vagaries of soil and climate, all its particular "conditions." The kind of language people use in articulating their world and dealing with one another. The habit of mind they bring to the contingencies of daily living: open and inquisitive about new possibilities, inventive, unafraid of failure, or anxiously hedged about by rules, traditions that no longer fit, fear of the uncontrollable and unknown. The temper that makes them choose this rather than that kind of state — federation for example: this or that form of nation. A stance that does not always need to live with certainty but is happy, or happy enough, with open questions, with unfolding time and the unfinished, with what is still "in the making"; that is curious about ends but happy in the meantime with the challenge and surprises of being "on the way."

This may sound abstruse, even vaporous, but it is in fact the condition in which Australians have lived rather successfully, and in great stability, for the major part of their history — and Canadians, too, I'd guess. We are down-to-earth people, rooted, as most people are, in the particularities of daily living. This is the *other* history, the interior history, of what we are and have achieved. It is where more happens and is decided than we recognize.

Three years ago we had a referendum in Australia to decide for or against a republic. It was meant to be a very simple decision. What the republicans were arguing for was what was called the minimalist option, an Australian head of state to replace the queen. It was the simplest piece of politics imaginable, and that was all it was, a change in the political sphere. The only emotional appeal was to national sentiment. The head of state would at last be one of *us*. At its crudest this became the slogan "A resident for president."

But there are no simple questions. As soon as you turn a question over to the people, it develops nuances, complexities, because actual men and women refer it back to their own experience, bring to it their own expectations. What appeared simple picks up on their contradictions and becomes complex.

The question failed, for the simple reason that the people saw nothing in it. If that's all a republic was, a change in the head of state, what was the point of it?

No attempt was made to ground the idea of a republic in people's experience; to attach it to the principles Australians had developed and for so long lived by, to see it as the natural embodiment of those principles. There was no suggestion that *res publica,* commonwealth, is just what it says it is: what belongs to that public life, the common good, that as citizens we all belong to, and share, beyond our purely private lives; that the republic is about shared concern and affection between its members, the business of fairness, justice, the meeting of needs.

Once all this had been subtracted and the whole question reduced to the simple political one of the head of state, people simply were not touched. As if a republic is defined only by its head of state! And this was important, because in the experience of many new migrants, who now make up some 30 percent of us, this was just the sort of false republic they had fled from, a political fiction based around a head of state and dedicated to the mystification of presidential power.

In the event, only one of the seven states and territories, Victoria, voted yes, and by the narrowest margin.

What I have wanted to talk about tonight is the fabric of things, that dense interweaving of lived experience that gives texture to our political lives and structures and determines the choices we make about where we are going, what is to endure, what is to change. Without this, political questions and choices have no urgency, because they have no relation to what we are.

Which leads me back to that moment in 1848 when the LaFontaine-Baldwin administration had to decide how they were to respond to mob violence and the challenge to elected government.

Their refusal to meet violence with violence was an attempt to pre-empt the future. To create, in the heat of the present, what might constitute, in time, a cool and usable past. To establish a pattern of behaviour that the people would recognize as both practical and as a reflection of their own temper.

What was decided at the moment was that in this society authority would neither be established nor maintained by violence, and that conflict would not be resolved by violence.

These moments when the temper of a society is defined and shown are decisive. It is these patterns of behaviour, this temper, more than any form of government that in the end determines the kind of society we create; how far it conforms to the common good; how, from one century to the next, it can be referred back to, and kept true to its own best self.

Louise Arbour

∿ 6TH ANNUAL LAFONTAINE-BALDWIN LECTURE

Le Capitole
Quebec City, Quebec
Friday, March 4, 2005

Introduction

In the fall of 1999, I was greatly honoured to receive the Eleanor and Franklin Roosevelt Institute's Freedom from Fear Award, in connection with my work as prosecutor for the International Criminal Tribunal for the Former Yugoslavia and for Rwanda.*

---

*I would like to express my gratitude to Jason Sigurdson and Mac Darrow in connection with the preparation of this address, and to Mara Bustelo and Dzidek Kedzia for their insights and sound advice. I must also pay tribute to my former law clerks in the Supreme Court of Canada, who shared some of my earlier thinking on these issues. Finally, thanks are due to Marc Gobeil from the office of John Ralston Saul and to Sue Adams from the library at the Coady International

On that momentous occasion, I found myself feeling envious of one of my co-honourees, who was being granted the Freedom from Want prize for that year. I had an intuition that hers would be harder to get.

I want to explore with you today why I think this is so. And I must state at the outset that although my reflection has been greatly enriched by my few months in office as the United Nations High Commissioner for Human Rights, I don't speak today in that capacity. I speak as a Canadian, as a Quebecer, but as one who always had a foot somewhere else.

Few ideas have been more powerful and influential than Franklin Delano Roosevelt's Four Freedoms. With tyranny unfolding across Europe, Roosevelt in his State of the Union address in January 1941 articulated a vision of four interconnected freedoms indispensable for a just and secure world: freedom from fear, freedom from want, freedom of speech and expression, and the freedom of religious worship. These freedoms captured the global imagination and came to be enshrined in the human rights compact among nations: the United Nations Charter (1945), the Universal Declaration of Human Rights (1948) and the legally binding human rights treaties that have followed.

Roosevelt predicted — optimistically, as events have transpired — that the fulfillment of the four freedoms would be achievable within one generation. While such goals have proven elusive in the twentieth, it has not been for a lack of resources. Despite our growing global base of financial and human capital,

Institute in Antigonish, Nova Scotia, as well as to Émile and Nicole Martel, who have facilitated the passage of my ideas from one language to another.

increasingly sophisticated technology and the experience of decades in international co-operation, poverty, inequality and repression continue to fuel security threats both within societies and across borders. Globalization, although making good on certain of its promises to generate higher rates of economic growth, confers the vast majority of its benefits on a chosen few.

According to data published by the World Bank (2004), the average level of real income in the richest countries is fifty times that of the poorest. Where there is social and economic inequality, people experience profound differences in access to political power, access to justice and access to the goods and social conditions that support well-being more broadly: food, shelter, healthy environments and health care. Democratic institutions can seem frail against the growing power and influence of multinational corporations, international organizations and other external actors. Such fundamental security challenges are not just for individual nation-states to face alone. They require international co-operation, and they are the subject of continuing debate and dialogue in international forums. That said, they require action, first and foremost, at home.

For its own part, Canada has consistently portrayed itself as an active promoter and defender of international human rights, and has, no doubt, displayed a strong commitment to multilateral approaches to global problems. It is a commitment that has, moreover, come to be a matter of national identity. Canadians have long identified with the blue beret of a UN peacekeeper, for example, in large part owing to the involvement of former prime minister Lester B. Pearson, Canada's sole Nobel Peace Prize Laureate, in the creation of a UN peacekeeping force during the 1956 Suez Crisis.

What about the case of human rights at home? The values of freedom, equality and tolerance reflect a very large consensus in Canada. They are values that have been entrenched in the Constitution through the 1982 Charter of Rights and Freedoms, and embodied in our international commitments under the International Covenant on Civil and Political Rights, the International Covenant on Economic, Social and Cultural Rights and the Convention on the Elimination of All Forms of Discrimination against Women, among others. I want to ask you today, however — perhaps somewhat provocatively — if we have done everything within our power to give effect to those values, and those legal commitments, in our day-to-day life as a nation.

During the 1990s, as a nation we were quick to celebrate our number one ranking on the Human Development Index. The index is the UN Development Programme's annual comparative assessment of human well-being worldwide, assessed on indicators including life expectancy at birth, literacy and gross domestic product. It gives a snapshot of well-being at an aggregate level, but it is a long way from reflecting the experiences of a country's most vulnerable citizens.

Despite our international standing, however, it was evident that poverty and gross inequalities persisted in our own back-yard. And so, the Human Poverty Index tells a different story, where last year (2004) Canada could manage only a twelfth place ranking out of the seventeen OECD countries listed, a distressingly consistent pattern since the UNDP's rankings began. Other reports, studies and indicators, from home and abroad, reveal that First Peoples, single-parent families headed by women, persons with disabilities and many other groups continue to face conditions in this country that threaten their fundamental economic, social, civil, political and cultural human rights — the birthrights of all human beings under international law.

How can such glaring disparities prevail in a country such as this, a wealthy, culturally diverse, cosmopolitan democracy? What is it in Canadian society that prevents the poor and marginalized from claiming equal enjoyment to the full range of their rights recognized under law, including economic, social and cultural rights? Can such entrenched marginalization really be dismissed as the fault of the marginalized, as some would tacitly suggest? To what extent can we point to shortcomings in our democratic processes or legal system? Or do such anomalies compel us towards a deeper examination of the basic values for which Canadians purport to stand?

It is impossible, I believe, to gain a full appreciation of the Canadian human rights experience, or to fully understand our values and our history, de-linked from the international legal and political context of which the Canadian experience forms an inextricable part. I would like, therefore, to take one step back, and look at the core ideas and values that underpin the international human rights system, highlighting Canada's role in the process. This should help us to better understand the evolution of Canadian political history and legal culture — and ultimately, our very partial and hesitant embrace of economic, social and cultural rights.

Canada and the International Origins of Economic, Social and Cultural Rights

As important as it is to international human rights law as we know it today, our collective interest in human dignity and well-being did not originate with the Universal Declaration of Human Rights. "Welfare rights" in general can be traced to two major political and socio-economic phenomena: the rise of nation-states and their evolution into mass democracies after the French Revolution, on the one hand, and the emergence of capitalism as the dominant mode of production following the Industrial Revolution, on the other. Within these two sets of transformations, welfare rights and institutions could be seen as responding to nascent demands for social security and income equality, with the perceived legitimacy of the state itself coming to depend at least in part upon its ability and willingness to meet these demands. In this sense, the welfare state can be understood as an accommodation and compromise between economic imperatives and socio-political demands.

No doubt, the priority that we choose to attach to different rights reveals much about the rich array of political and cultural traditions the world over. The Western bias today towards a particularly narrow strand of "civil liberties" likely has more to do with their instrumentality for neoliberal, market-driven policy imperatives than anything else. Such policy preferences, however, do not warrant subjugating — or obfuscating — rights labelled "socio-economic" for their supposed incompatibility with liberalism or the so-called rules of the market. To do so would require turning a blind eye to not only the shared historical origins of many of these rights, but also to the close conceptual and functional connectedness between them. I wish to underscore that my own use of "categories" when talking about particular rights from here onwards is only to address the distinction drawn by others.

Roosevelt's four interlinked freedoms captured the global imagination. The story of the Universal Declaration, and the place of socio-economic rights within it, reflected an integrated vision of the human being, embodying the interests and entitlements necessary for a life with dignity. This story is in great part a Canadian one. The task of drafting the declaration was officially that of the newly constituted Commission on Human Rights, meeting for the first time in New York in 1947. The commission was chaired by Eleanor Roosevelt, a strong advocate for economic, social and cultural rights. René Cassin, representing France, was later to receive the Nobel Peace Prize for his contributions to the Universal Declaration and Covenant drafting processes. However, it fell to the director of the Human Rights Division of the commission's Secretariat, Canadian John P. Humphrey, to produce a first draft of the Universal Declaration, taking into account drafts and submissions from member states and expert bodies.

Humphrey, having taught law at McGill University for almost ten years, entered the United Nations Secretariat on August 1, 1946, and retired more than twenty years later. He later described his own role as a "behind the scenes one," although no doubt his personal contribution was an important one. Humphrey attached great personal importance to socio-economic rights, drawing inspiration from the work of legislators the world over.

While Cold War rivalry was later to frustrate efforts to negotiate a single legally binding covenant covering all human rights, this was no barrier during the period 1947–48. Spurred by the power of the Four Freedoms idea, the inclusion of a wide spectrum of human rights within the declaration was achieved with tacit advance agreement. Naturally, the spectre of World War II was in clear view too, influencing the elaboration of all rights, including those of a "socio-economic" character.

The Canadian relationship with the genesis of the declaration is not defined by Humphrey's role alone. Considered by many to be one of our greatest political figures, Lester B. Pearson was an equally noted protagonist in the story of the declaration. This may hardly seem surprising in view of the social policy developments that took place during the 1950s and 1960s under Pearson's watch. These included the introduction of the Canada Pension Plan and family assistance plan, and — despite fierce opposition from insurance companies and some of the provinces — a national system of universal medicare. He was also later to establish the Royal Commission on Bilingualism and Bicultural-ism, and the Royal Commission on Women, which led to sweeping changes in the place and role of women in Canadian society. Pearson also introduced other landmark progressive policy initiatives in the field of education, including a system of student loans to provide greater opportunity for young Canadians to go to university. His initiatives extended to labour and immigration policy as well, and, in academic life, following his retirement, he led a major study advocating increased aid for the developing world. During a distinguished political career, he achieved the most sweeping and progressive package of legislation ever put before Canadians, and he did it without incurring a deficit.

However, Pearson's imprint as a newly appointed secretary of state for External Affairs in 1948 was not what a casual observer of history, with knowledge of his subsequent work, might expect. Indeed, Canada's entire role in the genesis of the Universal Declaration came to be mired in political intrigue and controversy. Canada's position on socio-economic rights, in particular, varied from ambivalence to outright hostility.

The low watermark in Canada's international stance on social and economic rights occurred towards the final stages of the negotiation process on the draft declaration, when Canada — led by Prime Minister Louis St. Laurent and Pearson — elected to abstain from a critical vote on the declaration in the committee of the UN General Assembly charged with human rights issues, one of only a small handful of countries to do so. While ultimately Canada did vote in favour of the declaration in the full General Assembly, the initial abstention decision embarrassed Canada internationally and, in the words of Professor William Shabas, "left a blemish that fifty years have not erased." This is hardly the story we might imagine given our national self-perception.

The reasons for the abstention related very directly to misgivings that prevailed then in official circles in Canada at the inclusion of socio-economic rights in the declaration. In Pearson's statement to the General Assembly on December 10, 1948, however, the true nature of these misgivings was not apparent on the face of his words. Rather, Pearson challenged the vague and "imprecise" nature of the language used in the draft declaration, and he noted that Canada had abstained on certain articles — notably, the right to education and the right to cultural life — on the basis that these matters were within provincial rather than federal jurisdiction. While it is true that there were provincial administrations that were concerned about federal interference, the stated justifications for the Canadian abstention simply do not hold up to critical scrutiny. It was very clear that St. Laurent was under pressure from conservative elites, including members of the Canadian Bar Association, who wanted to see an abstention. His intervention was crafted accordingly.

In his diaries, Humphrey described Pearson's statement to the General Assembly on December 10, 1948, as "one of the worst contributions," and a "niggardly acceptance of the

Declaration because it appeared [that] the Canadian government did not relish the thought of remaining in the company of
those who, by abstaining in the vote, rejected it." More point-
edly, Professor Shabas asserts that the provincial jurisdiction
concerns were mere pretext for avoiding human rights commitments: "The Canadian Government, and the Department of
Foreign Affairs in particular, misled both domestic and international public opinion by concealing its substantive opposition
to the Declaration behind procedural arguments."

In the ensuing years Canada joined other Western states in
thwarting aspirations for a single international treaty embracing
all rights in the Universal Declaration. The result was the development of two separate covenants and the consequent construc-
tion of an artificial boundary between the rights concerned: civil
and political on one side, economic, social and cultural on the
other. While we've seen some notable advances in the recognition of social and economic rights in Canada in recent years, the
ambivalent echoes of Pearson's words on Human Rights Day,
December 10, 1948, still reverberate within our political and
legal cultures today, part of an enduring reluctance to give effect
to economic, social and cultural rights. For such a generous
people, such reluctance strikes me as puzzling, to say the least.

Economic, Social and Cultural Rights
in Canadian Political and Legal Culture

Thinking in terms of Canada's social history, it is well worth
remembering that the early to mid twentieth century is not a
bygone era of co-operation and solidarity. Social transformations demand political commitment, often generated by the

work of Canadians — individually and together — who work for their ideals, who hold politicians to account and who defend principles wherever they are, whether it's the kitchen table or the international stage. From where I am today, I am particularly interested both in the local roots and the outside influences that have shaped our approach to social and economic rights. Allow me to turn briefly and selectively to a few events and personalities from the twentieth century that help put the contemporary pursuit of "freedom from want" in context.

I want to start in the Maritimes with Dr./Rev. Moses Coady and the Antigonish Movement, which has become synonymous with his name. While historical shorthand tells us that the 1930s were "dirty" and the '20s were "roaring" — a boom time preceding the stock market crash of 1929 — rural Nova Scotia knew nothing of this distinction. Before and after the crash, the situation for Maritimers was dire. The plight of fishing communities was brought to the attention of the federal government following a public meeting held in Canso on Dominion Day in 1927, the diamond jubilee of Confederation. The call for action prompted the government to appoint a Royal Commission to investigate the fishing industry. Among its recommendations, the commission stated that Maritime fisherfolk should be organized. Dr. Coady was appointed to take on this job.

Dr. Coady's plan centred on adult education and economic co-operation for the purposes of conquering poverty and creating the "good and abundant life." The key to freedom from want rests in collective action. Together with his colleagues from the Extension Department at St. Francis Xavier University, Coady took this message from town to town, touching the lives of more than fisherfolk and their families. Coal miners and

farmers, having no shortage of their own difficulties in shelter-
ing, feeding and clothing their families, came to the same study
clubs that Coady helped set in motion. Coady's message was not
a palliative taste of hope but rather a call to action.

Where did Coady's ideas come from? While the Antigonish
Movement later received international attention as a model for
community economic development, it is worth remembering
that there were outside influences. The idea of the "study club"
was something that Coady imported from Sweden. Even in the
early 1900s, people were taking notice of ideas that might have
local application — such a global perspective is not merely a
product of our globalized contemporary world.

Leonard Marsh was another figure in the history of
Canadian social policy development who kept an eye on developments abroad. Working under the direction of former McGill
University principal F. Cyril James, Marsh served as research
director of the Committee on Post-War Reconstruction. He was
largely responsible for the *Report on Social Security for Canada* in
1943. It set out a blueprint for a welfare state that would ensure
that there were collective benefits available to meet the needs of
Canadians at every point in the lifecycle. It advocated a
minimum set of social entitlements and called for the eradica-
tion of poverty. While many Canadians are acutely aware of the
divergent paths of Americans and Canadians on any number of
contemporary social issues, it is worth remembering that it was
not so long ago that the cue for expanding social programs was
taken from the United States. Commentators have noted that in
addition to being a student of William Beveridge, the designer
of Great Britain's post-war welfare state, Marsh was also inspired
by the ability of the Roosevelt administration to respond to the
dire consequences of the Great Depression of the 1930s. In

essence, the Four Freedoms, far from being only a part of the American story or even the Universal Declaration's story, were also part of the Canadian story.

It probably is not surprising that the same people who were skeptical about economic, social and cultural rights in the context of an international declaration on human rights were also less than enthusiastic about Marsh's recommendations. Political scientist and welfare state scholar Antonia Maioni points out that "the content and provenance of Marsh's report were enough to generate a great deal of hostility, not to mention embarrassment, on the part of Mackenzie King and his Liberal cabinet." The prime minister worried about the extent of fiscal pressures that would be placed on the state. Maioni notes that the Marsh report received considerable scrutiny from the media and protests from the business community prior to being "hastily buried away."

Even if the recommendations in the Marsh report were not acted upon immediately, it was clear that they resonated with Canadians. In many respects they could be seen in the campaign of Tommy Douglas and the Cooperative Commonwealth Federation in Saskatchewan. Douglas was elected in 1944 after leading a campaign that ran under the banner "Humanity First." His platform was true to the principles and vision espoused at the founding convention of the CCF, held in Regina eleven years prior to that victory. Delegates at the convention expressed their commitment to the retention and extension of social legislation, the socialization of health services, and federal responsibility for the unemployed. It was clear to Douglas that social services were special types of goods, not commodities that could be made contingent on the ability to pay. This was a social, political and moral commitment. And it was also a personal commitment, from someone who knew that it was only the charity of a doctor that saved his leg from amputation during his youth. Charity is a wonderful thing, but we also know — as Douglas knew then — that it is better to give than to receive.

Under Douglas's leadership, the province moved quickly to establish a provincial hospital care program, the first of its kind in the country. There were no limits on length of stay, only the need for the assurances of a medical doctor that the hospital stay was medically required. Mental health care was included. Seniors were insured not only for hospital care, but also for dental care and eyeglasses. Politically, health care was widely considered as having the status of an entitlement. Increasingly the same could be said elsewhere in the country.

Today we might take it for granted that it is a cherished national institution, something we see as a cornerstone of Canadian values, a way of honouring our fundamental commitment to each other. In discussing progress, however, we should not lose sight of the fact that the establishment of systems of public, universal health insurance and health care was a controversial and contested development in its time. The adoption of the Saskatchewan Medical Care Act on Canada Day, 1962, prompted a twenty-three-day doctors' strike in the province. Thousands came out to the steps of the legislature in Regina. The media reported that there was talk of possible violence. Doctors, some of medicare's most ardent defenders today, were less likely to back the government's pursuit of a single-payer, publicly provided health care system. In an interview with the CBC, the vice-president of the Saskatchewan College of Physicians and Surgeons at the time stated that "There's no doubt that you can not order charity, you can not order mercy, you can not order good motives and good feeling towards your fellow man." While his comments are perhaps accurate in their narrowest sense, I would argue that society can build institutions that embody and reinforce all those values, and, moreover, that there is a legal obligation to do so that goes to the core of the protection and promotion of human dignity.

Subsequent events tell us that Canadians saw that potential, too. Building on support for Saskatchewan's policies and program, the federal government aimed to create a plan that would extend protection to all Canadian citizens. In 1964, a report from the Royal Commission on Health Services was tabled by Supreme Court Justice Emmett Hall. He recommended a joint federal/provincial system that would cover the costs of preventative health care services and hospital care for all Canadians. In 1967, a national mechanism for the financing of health care was created, and the last provinces signed on in 1972. In all that transpired, it would seem that the federal government had finally overcome the sensitivities about intruding into the areas of provincial jurisdiction that it expressed so forcefully as a basis for its resistance to social, economic and cultural rights in the Universal Declaration in 1948.

The most dramatic example of social transformation can likely be found in the Quebec experience of the 1960s: the Quiet Revolution saw the rapid expansion of the état-providence, when health, education and social services left the hands of the church and became public, secular institutions administered by the Government of Quebec. The Quiet Revolution was about more than the secularization of social institutions, however. It was a social project that aspired to challenge old elites and create new relationships of justice. While it drew on the energies of young intellectuals and journalists, commentators have observed that one could still see roots that drew on the philosophy of social Catholicism, as well as Keynesian liberalism. It is also worth noting that the movement was careful to preserve aspects of the province's culture and that it reflected the linguistic and religious protections found in the British North America Act of 1867. The establishment of the *Commission Parent* on education led to the adoption of a secular education system that retained its historical Catholic or Protestant character.

In a few short decades, Canadians and their political leaders seemed to grow to embrace collective responses to meeting each other's needs, when it came time to raise a family, as well as in times of unemployment and disability, in sickness and in old age. What was the essential nature of the choices being made and the goods being dealt with? Public policy decisions were reflected in law, regulations and institutions, but, ultimately, the decisions remained political choices, and as political choices go, they remained subject to reversal. The adoption of the Canadian Charter of Rights and Freedoms in 1982 held the potential to change in a fundamental way the relationship between the executive, legislature and judiciary as we knew it, opening up the possibility for an articulation of the rights-based component of public policy decisions. Section 7, guaranteeing the right of everyone to life, liberty and security of the person, is particularly relevant in the context of "freedom from want." Political scientists and legal scholars watched the courts with great interest to see what the impact of judicial review on public policy decisions would be.

The first two decades of Charter litigation testify to a certain timidity — both on the part of litigants and the courts — to tackle head-on the claims emerging from the right to be free from want. This may have been caused, in part, by the three-year moratorium on equality rights, which therefore received constitutional protection only after the judiciary had had an opportunity to flex its intellectual muscles on the more familiar and less challenging claims related essentially to fairness in the criminal justice system. Equality rights were perceived, like social and economic rights, to invite broader social engineering, and to generate more conflict between legal demands and political accommodation.

Looking back at the discussion on the place of economic and social rights in the Universal Declaration, some might then observe that not much has changed with regard to the conversation on these rights in Canada today. Given the dramatic transformation of our social protection infrastructure during this same period, this stagnation seems odd, to say the least. In their social affairs, Canadians will affirm values strongly and publicly — in fact, even the recent Royal Commission on the Future of Healthcare in Canada called its final report "Building on Values" — but, strangely, there is a reticence to give those values the force of law and full-fledged constitutional protection. Canadian courts have championed civil and political rights and have articulated for themselves an appropriately far-reaching sphere of judicial review when the state invokes the use of repressive criminal law powers. But considerably more reticence has been expressed in relation to social, economic and cultural rights and the protection of vulnerable segments of the population on grounds other than discrimination.

The approach of Canada's courts has not escaped the notice of the United Nations Committee on Economic, Social and Cultural Rights. In 1998, when reviewing Canada's compliance with its international obligations, the committee stated that it had received information about a number of cases in which claims were brought by people living in poverty, alleging that government policies denied the claimants and their children adequate food, clothing and housing. The committee noted that provincial governments "have urged upon their courts ... an interpretation of the Charter which would deny any protection of Covenant rights and consequently leave the complainants without the basic necessities of life and without any legal remedy." It is important to stress that the committee is not stating that governments have an obligation to directly provide all things to all peoples. What it has pointed out, however, is that courts in Canada have "routinely opted for an interpretation of the Charter which excludes protection of the right to an adequate standard of living and other Covenant rights."

Very public, worldwide criticism of this nature is, of course, very hard to take. One might argue that it is even harder to take in the context of public — bordering on enthusiastic — commitments Canada has made under the banners of solidarity and social justice. It is the sign of a mature democracy, however, for a country to respond with professionalism and continued commitment to participating in those international mechanisms of accountability. There is, after all, limited benefit to be derived from isolated self-congratulations.

Ultimately, the potential to give economic, social and cultural rights the status of constitutional entitlement represents an immense opportunity to affirm our fundamental Canadian values, giving them the force of law. It honours the commitments made by Canadian legislatures when they ratified international human rights instruments. Of course, courts and human rights instruments do not purport to have all the answers on all of the most important social and political questions of the day, and it is simply beyond the capacity of the courts to adjudicate on every single matter with a human rights implication.

But just because the questions contain a substantial political dimension does not mean that they are beyond the reach of the judiciary, as I'll shortly discuss.

International Perspectives

Whatever cause there may have been to question the equal status and justiciability of economic, social and cultural rights sixty years ago, one thing is clear: there is no basis for categorical disclaimers today. The equal status, indivisibility and interdependence of all human rights have been affirmed unanimously and repeatedly by the international community of states, most notably at the Vienna World Conference on Human Rights (1993) and in 2000 at the Millennium Summit. Socio-economic rights have the status of binding law under a multitude of international human rights treaties, some enjoying near universal ratification, as well as in the Inter-American, African and European regional human rights systems, where procedures are in place to ensure that violations of these rights are redressed.

Roosevelt's "freedom from want," borne through the Universal Declaration of Human Rights, now breathes life into dozens of constitutions from all regions of the world, from South Africa, to France, to Finland, India, Syria, Romania, Argentina, Nigeria, the Philippines, Sri Lanka, Papua New Guinea and Bangladesh.

As is the case for civil and political rights, economic and social rights may — and in many circumstances must — be backed by legal remedies. Courts the world over have been playing an increasingly vital role in enforcing socio-economic rights, within the bounds of their justiciability, bringing them from the realms of charity to the reach of justice.

In 2001 in India, the Supreme Court made a legal claim to the right to food as an integral element of the right to life. South Africa provides another notable example in the context of the right to health. While political avenues failed, the Treatment Action Campaign launched a successful challenge in the South African Constitutional Court, obtaining an order that required the government to make anti-retroviral medication available to pregnant women living with HIV and AIDS so as to more effectively prevent mother-to-child transmission of HIV. In Argentina, there is a similar story to be told, with the courts ordering the government to take reasonable and affordable measures to address a hemorrhagic fever endemic to the country.

These examples show how social mobilization, judicial review and political action can vindicate rights, with potential life-saving impacts, when they are implemented together. In this sense, I believe there are important lessons for Canada here. The realization of economic and social rights is inherently a political undertaking, involving negotiation, disagreement, trade-offs and compromise. But political processes do not serve all equally. Equality requires, among other things, that the most disadvantaged be empowered to participate meaningfully both in political and legal processes, unshackling them from the benevolence and whim of the powerful, and enabling them to control their own destinies.

Securing implementation of court orders in human rights cases has often proven a challenge, but such challenges only underscore the importance of seeing litigation strategies as part of a broad, participatory movement for social change. In this, we see how all human rights are indivisible and interrelated.

Economic, social and cultural rights claims cannot be vindicated in the absence of minimum civil and political rights guarantees: freedom to organize, access to information on the entitlements in question, access to the judicial system. And the same applies vice versa.

The experiences in India, South Africa, Argentina and elsewhere help to dispel categorical assertions as to the non-justiciability of socio-economic rights. In principle and in practice, there are justiciable elements in most if not all human rights reflected in the Universal Declaration. Based on comparative experience, the prospects for effective judicial enforcement depend more upon the authority of the courts hearing the claim than on anything inherent in the nature of the right in question.

International and national-level jurisprudence also helps us to better understand the substantive content of economic, social and cultural rights, and the limits of entitlements and obligations arising thereunder. With the international standards and experience in view, it is impossible to regard socio-economic rights obligations as fanciful or far-fetched. Human rights of all kinds involve *freedoms* as well as *entitlements*. Each kind of obligation may have cost implications to varying degrees, be they for the infrastructure necessary for the administration of justice; the human and technical resources necessary to regulate financial or social sectors; or the direct provision of water, sanitation, housing or other services as needed. Human rights law insists on principle, rationality and equity in the process of resource allocation, and on moving steadily forward within the prevailing resource constraints. While the standard of achievement for all countries is the same, the national benchmarks will differ greatly. However, whatever the resource constraints, there is a core minimum international legal obligation to secure a floor of rights and services beneath which people should never be allowed to fall.

Both in principle and in practice, the realization of social and economic rights is not predicated upon any particular political or economic system, although the extremes at either end of the ideological spectrum are unlikely to be favourable. The fact that social and economic rights have been litigated successfully in many different legal systems helps to bear this out. Allegations as to the uniformly and uniquely "costly" nature of socio-economic rights obligations seem at best strange or misinformed, or at worst, disingenuous, set against these realities. The barriers to rational debate on these matters are probably better explained by underlying ideological preferences, especially those associated with the libertarian ideal of a minimalist state. Liberty and political freedoms, as much as basic socio-economic entitlements, depend on taxes. In most instances, expenditures on human rights enforcement is money well spent. Girls' education has been proven to be the best long-term investment that there is. Security of tenure, women's rights and participation rights all have demonstrably major development dividends. Conversely, recent World Bank research casts doubt on whether sustained increases in economic growth are achievable with declining distributional equity.

The real issue is not regulation or state action in and of itself, but, rather, *what* is being regulated, and in the interests of *whom:* the market, national elites, the aggregate interest of the majority, or the disadvantaged and the vulnerable. Poverty and exclusion are too readily accepted by majorities as regrettably accidental, or natural or inevitable, rather than the outcome of conscious policy choices. All underlying agendas and preferences must be brought to the surface if these debates are to lead to policy decisions that produce just outcomes.

Of course there will always be those who object to an active judicial role in regulating public and private life, especially where the effect of court action runs counter to current majoritarian will. But in truth, in addressing human rights claims, judges generally display a very clear regard for the proper preserve of elected legislatures. The substantive tasks involved in reviewing social and economic rights claims are no quantum leap from those associated with ordinary judicial review functions, such as examining the "reasonableness" of official conduct in accordance with objective criteria. In many cases it has been sufficient for courts to find that particular groups of people are being unfairly discriminated against under social benefits schemes, or that governments have failed to implement existing (reasonable) laws and policies.

The legality of judicial review of all human rights is not open to question under the Canadian constitutional system. The legitimacy of a constitutional interpretation that reflects the universality and indivisibility of all human rights expressed in international instruments ratified by Canada should also not be open to question. Early in the history of the Charter, there was skepticism towards judicial remedies for the denial of fundamental rights both from those who feared an overly timid judiciary and from those who dreaded overly ambitious courts. Would constitutional supremacy lead to politics being superseded by legalism, politicians by lawyers, parliamentarians by judges, the reality of power by the rhetoric of rights?

In my view, both extreme forms of skepticism proved ill-founded. Courts are well-equipped to reflect the entrenched expectation of Canadians that equitable access to the riches generated by our collective harvesting of this generous land is no longer a matter of charitable disposition.

Work is advancing at the international level to promote the justiciability of economic, social and cultural rights, and there are key opportunities to take leadership on this issue. In recent years United Nations member states have been examining options for the elaboration of an Optional Protocol to the International Covenant on Economic, Social and Cultural Rights. Depending on the shape it is given, an Optional Protocol could give rise to a legal mechanism that would allow individuals to bring their claims to an international forum, in cases where national recourse has been found wanting. This is an important development in international law, one that promises to help parties to the covenant honour the commitments they have made at law, complementing and expanding remedial avenues under the European, Inter-American and African regional human rights systems, and affirming our deeper social commitment to the realization of a life of dignity for all people. Creating such an instrument is an expression, not an abrogation, of state sovereignty. The decisions that need to be taken clearly belong to states. As a Canadian, however, it is my personal hope that Canada will play a leadership role in future discussions, projecting a moral voice that mobilizes and galvanizes international support for such a protocol and all that it represents.

Conclusion

Human rights embody an international consensus on the minimum conditions for a life of dignity. But human rights are not a utopian ideal. At any given point in time, they must be understood as the product of a struggle — whether made explicit or otherwise — between and within states, over ideas, ideologies, politics and resources. It is the interplay of these forces and the outcomes of these struggles that influence the textual formulations and formal interpretations of human rights, as well as the prospects for their vindication through legislative, political and judicial processes. The reason that "rights talk" is resisted by the powerful is precisely because it threatens (or promises) to rectify distributions of political, economic or social power that, under internationally agreed upon standards and values, are unjust.

These truths are laid bare in Canada's very hesitant recognition and selective implementation of some of its international human rights obligations. But sixty years of disclaiming or belittling the equal status of socio-economic rights as enforceable human rights, fundamental to the equal worth and dignity of all Canadians, rings hollow and disingenuous in the light of international and comparative experience. There is nothing to fear from the idea of socio-economic rights as real, enforceable, human rights on equal footing with all other human rights, and no cause for simplistic or categorical distinctions between these rights, and rights described as "civil and political." Human rights obligations require nothing more or less than reasonable efforts within the maximum extent that resource constraints permit, with priorities determined through inclusive democratic processes, and with an abiding concern for the situation of the most disadvantaged.

The possibility for people themselves to claim their human rights entitlements through legal processes is essential so that human rights have meaning for those most at the margins, a vindication of their equal worth and human agency. There will always be a place for charity, but charitable responses are not an effective, principled or sustainable substitute for enforceable human rights guarantees. The debate in Canada on these issues will certainly continue. However, those who fear or object to the vision of human rights that I've outlined would do well to bring the true nature of their misgivings into the open, out from under the shadows of straw men and calculated obfuscation. If we engage on the substantive issues in good faith, I believe that there will be a more just, inclusive and rights-respecting democracy in Canada in years to come, and that we shall be able to project abroad an unambiguous Canadian vision of the world.

∾ CONVERSATION TWO

JOHN RALSTON SAUL: *Values* is a word we hear used a great deal, and I'm never sure what it means. It could be positive or negative. It could be an aspect of old-fashioned negative nationalism. I know you have all used it carefully. So I wonder what you make of this sudden fashion for *values*.

BEVERLEY MCLACHLIN: *Values* has come to mean nothing because it means so much. It has a special meaning in the legal lexicon, where we will analyze a legal problem that involves a conflict of interest by saying, "These are the values on this side, and these are the values on the other," such as freedom of speech on one side or equality on the other. But then it has quite a different meaning in the political sense, where it means whatever you think is really important, and that could be diametrically different things, depending on your perspective.

LOUISE ARBOUR: Inevitably, what *values* means is always positive. We never talk about bad ideas, we don't say that stereotypes reflect values. So the word helps us to organize a discourse or a balance of all good things, all positive things. In that sense, when John said that values could encompass, for instance, old-fashioned nationalism, I think you meant it not in a positive fashion.

JOHN RALSTON SAUL: Yes, let's say a nineteenth-century concept of nationalism, which includes *values* as an expression of "I'm-better-than-you" exclusion.

DAVID MALOUF: When the word *values* comes up, the suggestion is that either a person, or the society as a whole, has failed to live up to some kind of values that were once there. This comes up very strongly from politicians, who often talk about the way certain kinds of values existed, say, in the 1950s. The suggestion is that honesty is disappearing from our society, mostly in the realm of politics. I don't know what it's like in Canada, but it has come up in our election in Australia; it came up in the election in the United States and in England, of a failure of trust in the prime minister. That suggests there were these values that once existed in politics that have now somehow slipped away.

When people juggle with that accusation, I'm not sure they know that people were more honest back then, or fairer or less selfish. It's really a way of talking about some kind of ideal that you wish people would live up to and that you feel we are not living up to, because life is now very complex. Also, because our societies are so varied, it's very difficult to generalize about them. So any generalization of that kind is going to be false.

So I see the word being used almost always to point to a failure, or a lack of what was once there.

BEVERLEY MCLACHLIN: Whether it was actually there is something that's sometimes debated.

DAVID MALOUF: Absolutely!

BEVERLEY MCLACHLIN: But it does express this feeling that we should be better than we are, or things should be done differently than they are, that people have lost their values.

DAVID MALOUF: I see it coming up especially when it's turned against the electorate: that the electorate are now selfish, are now concerned only with commodities, their mortgage, their financial security or their social security. This is a move away from the way their parents might once have felt.

JOHN RALSTON SAUL: I find myself regularly involved in immigration and citizenship questions. Australia and Canada are among the only countries in the world that actively say — having made a lot of mistakes in the past — "We really only want you to come here if you're going to become a citizen." We're upset when people immigrate and don't try to become citizens as fast as possible.

I've just come from Germany and Holland, where they're caught in the middle of a psychodrama about why they would want people to come even though they need them to come, and what would it mean if they did let them become citizens. And what would they tell them about what being a citizen means.

In other words, whatever we think about our society, we have to deal with this question of values when we talk to people who are becoming Canadians. Often they don't have the background of our experiences — good and bad — over the last 150 years, of where we got it right and where we got it wrong. Theoretically, Canadians at some level have a sense of this experience.

So when you think about what you've just been saying, knowing that we take 250,000 immigrants a year and Australia takes — David, do you know?

DAVID MALOUF: Oh, 110,000 or so.

JOHN RALSTON SAUL: So big numbers by anybody's standards. What do we say to people arriving in Canada to become citizens to jump-start them into what theoretically others have been living? Or should we say nothing?

BEVERLEY MCLACHLIN: I think that one of the things we try to tell people in Canada is that you come here with the expectation that there'll be diversity, and that you will not only have to tolerate but respect and appreciate different cultures. This respect for diversity has itself become a transcendental value, that whatever your personal credos — and one is encouraged to continue them because we encourage multiculturalism, to some extent — you have to tolerate and respect diversity.

But the interesting discussion that may be beginning in Canada is, What are diversity's limits? Do we need the same basic criminal law for everybody? Do we need the same basic family law for everybody? Are there some things that, when you come in — in addition to this respect for diversity — you should commit to? I hear conversations like that around.

JOHN RALSTON SAUL: That's why I raised the question of values.

BEVERLEY MCLACHLIN: I think it's something we're going to have to debate. It's a real challenge for our society, which, unlike the European societies, has focused on this need to tolerate and respect diversity, everybody getting along together with their different cultures. We've encouraged different cultures to develop, but we haven't really asked ourselves what are the absolute basic minimums on which we ask everybody who's a Canadian citizen to agree.

LOUISE ARBOUR: Well, I'm not sure that this is a question of seeking a consensus on shared values. Another point I'd like to make about what we mean when we source our arguments or refer to values is that it tends to be backward-looking rather than forward-looking. It's by definition conservative because it speaks about what we have already acquired and shared. We could talk about new values, but that kind of value-based discourse is looking at our roots and shared consensus, and I suppose we may be saying to newcomers, "You should embrace these values."

Inasmuch as we talk about multiculturalism and pluralism and are embracing diversity, we are talking less in concrete terms about us embracing the ideas of the newcomers, but inviting them not to share. Essentially, yes, to share in a common project that is forward-looking, but that's not done through values. The value discourse is essentially anchored in something that is behind us. It's about looking back.

DAVID MALOUF: But it needn't be. We could say that, for example, the way we've given women a choice about whether they have a child is actually a change of values, but we would want to argue that it is also an increase of freedom and tolerance in the community. It's a change of values that's made us make that move. So values can also be forward-looking.

LOUISE ARBOUR: I'm not so sure that I would say it's a change of values. Eventually values may change, but in some cases it could be a change in the law, and I don't believe that all legislative arrangements have to be absolutely anchored in values.

DAVID MALOUF: Yes.

LOUISE ARBOUR: You may have a lot of issues dealing, for instance, with the concept of life — issues related to abortion, capital punishment and so on — where the law may not exactly reflect personally held or commonly held values in large segments of society, but where people are prepared to concede so that they could live under a legal infrastructure that is different, for instance, from the values reflected in their church, in their family, in their small cultural group.

But they're prepared to yield to something that at times coincides, and at times doesn't, with their values. That's the law, that's the rights and underpinning of legislative frameworks.

DAVID MALOUF: It's very easy to use values in that backward-looking way that suggests society has fallen away from something. Whereas we know that society now is based on a great deal more sensitivity to the differences between people and to people's different needs. And to that extent, society is a more open, tolerant and caring place than it was.

LOUISE ARBOUR: Let me give an example, as perhaps I wasn't articulating my point all that well. If you take the issue of sexual identity and sexual orientation, for instance, I'm not sure that where Canada situates itself now is a reflection of values that are profoundly different than values you might find elsewhere, but I believe that its legal analysis of the concept of discrimination has allowed Canada to situate itself somewhere that may or may not reflect a great shift in values.

It depends what you qualify as the value underpinning prohibition. You could say, for instance, Canada has not abandoned any of its "family values" by embracing the prohibition of discrimination on the basis of sexual orientation, but at the same time it has embraced a new value, or there is a competing value, which is equality.

DAVID MALOUF: Yes.

JOHN RALSTON SAUL: I guess it's the old philosophical system, in which societies tend to identify points, or people, or sentences, in the past. Louise, you used the Four Freedoms of Roosevelt, for example, and Beverley quoted a series — as did David — of things out of the past. Our tendency is to look for something in the past — either a moment or a declaration — that had in it a truth. The people who said it at the time may not have understood the implications down the road. As we go along, we keep realizing that in today's terms there was a truth in that original statement that expresses what we are trying to address or fulfill.

An example is the Address to the Electors of Terrebonne, 1840. There is a paragraph on immigration and citizenship by LaFontaine, which is a perfect expression of our approach towards immigration and citizenship today. It took us 120 years — to 1960 — before we actually acted in a manner that reflected the ideas stated by LaFontaine.

So, we are always struggling with ideas that are enunciated long before they happen to be put into effect.

BEVERLEY MCLACHLIN: I suppose that's the perceptive individual who somehow has a sense of how things might go, although not a very clear sense, so people — statesmen — struggle to articulate what may happen, what may accommodate the needs of the nation down the way. For example, the Americans early on decided they'd have separation of church and state, and that's being challenged now. But it's an interesting debate, an idea that has been articulated in many different ways throughout the centuries.

JOHN RALSTON SAUL: Here you have the most important country in the world, which very clearly in all its legal documents separates church and state, now being run as if the church were meant to lead the state.

LOUISE ARBOUR: That's another lecture!

JOHN RALSTON SAUL: It is a fascinating question, though, because it challenges the whole idea of values and references to the past. I don't know whether we should just drop it. What do you think?

BEVERLEY MCLACHLIN: I think we should drop it. I'm sorry for introducing it!

JOHN RALSTON SAUL: No, no, it's one of the most perplexing phenomena out there today.
    Let me ask a related question then. All three of you talked about fear: what fear does, where it comes from, how it can drive

people to do the wrong thing, whether it's racism or exclusion or the negative side of nationalism. It could be argued that today we are seeing a rise of fear, for a variety of reasons, in many countries. There are examples of it in Canada. There are examples of it in Australia. And this fear can have an effect on public policy.

All three of you in different ways are thinking about it. Louise, you have to think about why people are doing the things they shouldn't be doing. Beverley, you have to think about that in terms of Canada. And David, as a novelist, you write about it all the time. What is it that has brought this fear back? What is the origin of fear in societies like ours, societies that — however much we complain — are about as successful as societies could possibly be?

LOUISE ARBOUR: I was flying back from Colombia last night to New York, and was making some notes for a speech. My tentative title was "Human Rights and the Politics of Fear." I more and more believe that this is a very central concept, and very useful to look at. I'm currently engaged in the Secretary-General's reform agenda, in which he situated human rights — as he puts it — as the third pillar of the United Nations system. The other two are security and development. He says there can be no security without development, no development without security, and neither security nor development without human rights.

Security is freedom from fear, development is freedom from want. Human rights is cross-cutting, under both the aspiration to be safe and to be fed and to be secure in a development sense. So human rights cut across both civil and political rights and economic and social rights. I think what you find at the root of all this is essentially a kind of fear for survival.

And what we see currently is a lot of manipulation of a basic personal instinct — but a very strong social instinct as well — one that is the most easily vulnerable to manipulation for political purposes. By activating this idea that there is reason to be afraid, a lot of the current discourse preys on people's sense of insecurity to make them surrender a considerable portion of their liberty, of their generosity, of their spirit of inclusion.

Fear has a lot of very positive elements, including the fact that it brings immediate alertness. But it has a lot of very negative elements, the first one being that it tends to generate a premature, irrational response. And I think that analysis is just as true in political decision-making as it is on a canoe trip when you have to react suddenly to an unexpected event. We see the politics of exclusion very much preying on this idea.

BEVERLEY MCLACHLIN: We wonder about this in the national arena when we're talking about criminal law, as a judge. And I know Louise must have had this experience: you go to meetings and people — the general public, not lawyers — talk about how crime is rising, and violence is increasing and so on. But the statistics show — as they did in Ontario recently — that there's been a steady decline in violent crime in major urban areas in the last decade. And yet you even see political people whipping this fear up, and you also see the media doing it, for different reasons.

I think the political people, be they a police chief or whatever, can use it to justify stronger measures, maybe take away liberties, that kind of thing. But the media is interesting. I was talking with a journalist who said that for the six o'clock news they were told to get the F stories. I asked, "Well, what are the F stories?" And he replied, "The fear stories." He said, "Why on earth would you watch the six o'clock news unless you were afraid? You want to know what to be afraid of."

There's a lot of manipulation by a lot of people to make us afraid in our society, and I'm sure it happens in other societies in different and similar ways.

DAVID MALOUF: Both of those observations certainly apply to what I see in Australia. Our societies are maybe very vulnerable to insecurity in this way. They are very calm places where we don't have a history — in Australia, anyway — of violence. And we don't know what it is, either, that makes the society completely cohesive. And because that's an entirely mysterious thing — the way a society hangs together — we're terribly insecure about the things that might somehow destabilize it.

I think Australia has always been like that. But now there are various sources of insecurity presented to us. Terrorism is one; the entry of illegal migrants violating our boundaries is another; the entry of international crime is another, and even something like identity theft, which is a new terror that's spread among the people. These all play right into the hands of governments that are really quite interested in getting everything under control. And there's a tendency for bureaucracies — in Australia, certainly — to find new outlets for their activities in order to grow. Fear is very, very useful.

Many freedoms that we've taken for granted in the past now seem to be presented as negotiable, so that we will be secure. I think that's a very dangerous and disturbing phenomenon.

JOHN RALSTON SAUL: Can I take this one level — I don't know if it is lower or higher? Many people are noticing now in Europe that levels of anti-Semitism are highest in places where there are the fewest Jews. And levels of anti-immigration feeling tend to be highest where there are the fewest immigrants. For example, in Germany whenever they do a study, apparently they find in Bradenburg — where the immigration population is 3 percent, one of the lowest in the whole country — the highest anti-immigrant feeling. Let's call it an unconscious level of fear, or a need to be afraid.

So I'm asking the same question again, but from somewhere beyond the political or journalistic scope. The story about the six o'clock news is fundamentally true. And there is manipulation. But there is something beyond that which you must think about when you're trying to figure out what justice is, or what policy could be, or what truth and fiction is.

LOUISE ARBOUR: It has something to do with identity. As I think Beverly said, we see that frequently in criminal law reform. For instance, you can have a lot of information — whether it's from the six o'clock news or anywhere else — about statistics of very high levels of trafficking in children all over the world. You could hear that every day. And it has one level of resonance for most Canadians: they deplore it. They think it's terrible. But they don't feel threatened in an immediate way.

And then you might have one case of one child kidnapped in any part of Canada, a part that may be two thousand miles away from where you live, and the next day this may affect your willingness to support modifications in the criminal law that will restrict liberty.

What's the difference between the two? It's not the magnitude of the information that you have just received — one case as opposed to hundreds of thousands of cases — it's the immediacy of the appeal and its impact on your own sense of self-preservation. And that's what I mean by the politics of fear.

It's exactly the same thing in economic and social rights. Migration, as David mentioned, is a classic case of manipulation. But you also see it when politicians start talking about, for instance, a potential insolvency of a pension plan. It has more resonance in some segments of the population than in others, in particular for those concerned about their own position in the future. And this will trigger a willingness to go somewhere politically that otherwise you might not have rationally accepted. And usually, contrary to values, it tends to make you do things that otherwise you would not be willing to do in terms of embracing some reforms or changes in the law or in social policies.

JOHN RALSTON SAUL: Anyone else?

BEVERLEY McLACHLIN: I'm thinking about your question, John, why a quiet society that really knows very little of immigration, for example, or Jewish people, would have more fear than a group where they're confronting them all the time. I think it's the fear of the unknown, the human imagination setting up the big-bad-wolf-in-the-forest myth. There's something in the human imagination that wants to have something else out there that we don't really know to blame our troubles on. And the more concrete and human it gets, the less that tendency, because it becomes ordinary, they're just like us. And I think that is a factor in this complex problem.

JOHN RALSTON SAUL: David has a phrase, "Nothing defines a people more clearly than what they fear." All three of you address it. But knowing that we have this fear of the unknown, what can we do? One of you talks about the eternal problem of how do we imagine *the Other*, which is what you're saying, Beverley — if you can imagine the Other you won't be afraid, not if you can have empathy or can project yourself.

BEVERLEY McLACHLIN: Exactly.

JOHN RALSTON SAUL: What do you think we're not doing in our two societies — or in other societies — that we could be doing to confront the question, which we know will always be there, of fear? Which will undermine, if we don't confront it, law and political fairness.

BEVERLEY McLACHLIN: We've done pretty well in Canada, I think, on the immigration front and the melding of cultures. We've done it by education and by exposure, and people just being together in our large cities and realizing the richness that comes out of the mix. We've done it because historically we always thought that that was a good thing. And we weren't that afraid of it since we've been French and English for so long. We understood it's difficult, but it's okay, and it enriches everybody.

But I haven't thought much about how we meet the new fears, the fears of terrorism, the fears of violence; those fears that, if we're not careful, will really lead — drive — a legislative agenda that will take away our freedoms.

But one finds very little public discussion about these issues in the same way that we have had in-your-face kinds of public discussion about multiculturalism. And I think that we need to somehow bring them out in the open and demystify them if we can. But it's tough to get the press even interested in discussing the other side of a fear story concerning security or crime. And without the media to drive these things, it becomes all that more difficult to deal with them.

DAVID MALOUF: What it is we actually fear keeps changing in various ways. What doesn't change is the irrational nature of the fear, which I think is a very primitive thing.

BEVERLEY McLACHLIN: Absolutely.

DAVID MALOUF: Australians once might have feared isolation, but what they now actually fear are new ways in which their protective border — the ocean — can be violated, because space is now virtual. Identity theft — which seems to be the latest thing terrifying everybody — is such a nebulous thing. There's no face to it, and there's no person you can confront and see is, after all, human and therefore not to be feared.

We need those fears in some way. Or somebody needs them. There are people out there who use those fears to insist that what we thought of as our absolute freedom really does have to be limited now, in some way. And I find that very scary.

BEVERLEY McLACHLIN: Don't you have to rationalize the irrational, whatever the object of the fear is?

DAVID MALOUF: Exactly.

BEVERLEY McLACHLIN: That has to be the recipe. It's not easy to do.

DAVID MALOUF: You have to recognize first that the fear is always irrational. Even if there's a reason for it, the fear itself is irrational, and that's what you have to deal with.

LOUISE ARBOUR: Well, maybe I could be disagreeable on this point. When we say fear is irrational, I think we mean that it expresses itself as an emotion. But very often the fear reaction is perfectly rational. That is, even if you had time to control your emotion, you should react the same way because there's every reason to be afraid. It's a very natural response for self-preservation. It's that state of alertness and quick appreciation of danger or jeopardy.

There are a few points I'd like to make on the basis of what we've said so far. The first one is when we ask ourselves where we, as Canadians, situate ourselves on this kind of spectrum of responsiveness to fear manipulation. I think we have a really good recent pop-culture point of reference in Michael Moore's movie *Bowling for Columbine.* Moore tries to capture the essence of cultural differences between Canadians and Americans, for instance, on the possession and use of firearms. He relates this to actual violence by postulating that Canadians are not afraid, and that's the difference.

But what's really interesting is the metaphor he uses in the movie, which has become known worldwide, that Canadians don't lock their doors. It doesn't have to be literally true, but the metaphor is really interesting because it keeps coming back in Canadian culture. You find exactly the same metaphor in Gilles Vigneault's song "Mon Pays," where he says, "My father built a house that will receive all the people of the world because humans are of my race." It's the same notion of the open door, which again reflects at least our perception of our immigration history and our current policies. Even if that's not actually true, that we are not quite as receptive and inclusive as we think we are, the point is we think we are because this is not where our fears are. They are somewhere else.

My second point is —

JOHN RALSTON SAUL: I'll just interject before you go ahead. What you have just said is exactly the point that LaFontaine made in 1840 in his paragraph on immigration in his Address to the Electors of Terrebonne. It was almost word-for-word what you've just said.

LOUISE ARBOUR: But you see, it's not just immigration, it's also crime. It's evil not just outside, but evil in our midst. We have crimes, we have homicides, but again this metaphor that we don't lock our doors is a way of saying not that we are fearless — maybe we are — but I think more realistically that our fears are somewhere else. They're there to some extent, but, say, less so compared to others. And Michael Moore, in his typical exaggerated fashion, makes that case very well.

The other point I'd like to make is that I think there are different kinds of fears. Some are unspeakable, and others are what I call feel-good fears. That's the difference between national disasters, for instance, and genocides. It's absolutely remarkable how we have a fascination for tsunami-like events, earthquakes and so on, and how it triggers immediately not a good fear but a response of awe. It's almost admiration for how awesome this planet is. For some people it may have religious references, but it triggers in us, collectively, generosity, brotherliness, a feeling of connection with the victims.

As soon as you arrive at victims of man-made atrocities, like genocide — and, on a smaller scale, crime — the level of empathy is very reduced, and there's a real unwillingness to identify with the victim. You don't identify with a rape victim the same way you identify with the victim of a fire or a car accident.

Because you're projecting something about your own fears out there, you're willing to take on the fears that come from acts of God or natural disasters. But there's something unspeakable about the fear that another human being would do something to you.

I can't take it any further than that, it's a very half-baked notion, but I think the observation is correct. I'm not sure where the analysis leads.

JOHN RALSTON SAUL: That may be half-baked in legal terms, but it's not in philosophical terms.

BEVERLEY MCLACHLIN: It's very interesting.

JOHN RALSTON SAUL: I have one big double question and one small one. Given all that we've already said, there are two areas that all three of you dealt with. One has to do with the role of women in society, and the other has to do with the place of Aboriginals in society.

I'm struck that after more than a century of brilliantly and actively organized movements for women's rights — and I'm talking to two of the most powerful women in the world, and I live with a third one — it's amazing how slowly they've gone, how much remains to be done, how many blockages remain. And at the same time we could say that we haven't even been close to getting it right in Canada and Australia on Aboriginal questions for all that long, not nearly as long as on the role of women, but we're starting to get it right. Yet again enormous blockages remain.

So the double question is, What is it that holds us back? And secondly — and that's really the question — if we get it right, in a broader sense, what is this going to do to our society? If women are really playing fully their role, if Aboriginals are playing fully their role in society, is this going to change the way in which we think about fear, justice, rights and so on? Are these major pieces that could change the way our societies work if they become fully integrated?

BEVERLEY McLachlin: Well, I think I'll take a stab at the first question. The second one's much more difficult. It seems to me that the reason we have so much difficulty improving the situation for women and for Aboriginals is that the structures are deep in our society, and they're not easy to change. You can change laws, but you cannot change attitudes that easily about who has primary child-care roles, et cetera. I don't know whether that ties to the Aboriginals — there may be a different dimension there — but they may also have institutionalized problems. For example, we have reserves that Aboriginal people cling to and want, and yet on the other hand it results in a kind of ghettoization that presents other problems.

So the problems are not just neat and clear. They're woven into the very structure of our society, and that is much more difficult to change. Along with that, of course, goes religion and attitudes, and these are not just attitudes that are shared, for example, only by men where women are concerned, or only by non-Aboriginals where Aboriginals are concerned. We have developed a kind of unified society in which we've built in all of these things, and to move it on and either untangle it or develop a new weave is very difficult; it takes a long time.

I think we're moving in the area of women, and I think we're moving in the area of Aboriginal people, and probably as history goes we're moving fairly quickly. But from our perspective, it seems to take a great deal of time, and there's no magic, instant solutions.

By the same token, to the extent we change, since it's all embedded in society, society will change. How, I'm not sure, but it will change as we move towards more equality for women and to dealing with Aboriginal issues.

DAVID MALOUF: Those two things seem rather different to me.

JOHN RALSTON SAUL: Yes, I shouldn't have put them together. It's just that in our two societies, these are two such obvious areas of strategic blockage.

DAVID MALOUF: As I notice how things have changed over a number of years in Australia, the change in the lives of women has been quite extraordinary. It goes further than I have seen it in some other places. It is a question of child-rearing, to some extent. What I notice walking around the city, and what I notice among people I know, is how many men have now taken over the role of child-rearing, and they don't seem threatened by it.

You notice, for example, if you go into a supermarket in the inner city where I live, the number of times it's a man with two children and a stroller rather than a woman doing the shopping.

The other difficult area is where women get into positions of authority, and in both of these cases it really partly depends on the willingness of men to see their own role differently, and

MCNALLY ROBINSON BOOKSEL
1120 GRANT AVE
WINNIPEG MB

ID B4085766
STORE 4085766
SLIP# 3843

SALE $25.68

INTERAC DIRECT PAYMENT S
451901*******3700
PAYMENT FROM CHEQUING ACCOUNT

APPROVED AUTH 009052
SEQ#303001001249 00-001
JUN 7 2006   7:21 PM

THANK YOU

CUSTOMER COPY

not to feel threatened by that change. But I agree it's a very, very slow business.

The Aboriginal question in Australia seems to be very different. I think, once, Aboriginals in Australia represented the darkness people feared most, and if one was talking about fears of that particular country, the fear of facing Aboriginal people and their otherness was once very, very great. We no longer see Aboriginal people in that way. What we find much more difficult is to recognize in their way of doing things structures that are themselves admirable and very different from our own, and it's taken us a long time to actually recognize how an Aboriginal society is made. The difficulty in trying to improve the lives and status of Aboriginal people is that most of those structures have now broken down, and family dysfunction, the abuse of children, the abuse of substances, violence towards women are endemic in almost all of those Aboriginal societies. And the role that men would once have had in those societies has been completely destroyed. It's the women who now are seen to be very strong in holding them together. That seems to me to be a situation that is worse, almost, than it was twenty or thirty years ago.

LOUISE ARBOUR: I agree that we have to make a lot of distinctions between these two groups of equality-seekers. I'm in New York today to participate in the indigenous forum, which is a large gathering of worldwide indigenous communities. So I'm preoccupied also with these kinds of issues.

But there are a few things — broadly speaking — that we could look at as being common to these two particular groups of equality-seekers, women and indigenous people, and it's true, I think, of others.

First, we have to ask ourselves whether we are addressing their claims and their aspirations in a normative fashion, or in a kind of instrumental fashion. Let's start with women. Are we saying women should have equal access to power and wealth and so on because it's fair and just and a good thing itself that power and wealth be shared equally among all groups in society? To me, that's a kind of normative argument. Or are we prepared to engage in a kind of instrumental argument: it's good because if there are more women in power we will have different outcomes in legal reasoning and social policy development and so on?

We have to ask ourselves which one we're talking about. We could advance the argument on both fronts, but we should always be clear as to which one we are making, because the indicators of measuring whether we are correct are very different, if we're having a normative discourse, or if we're using a sort of equality as instrumental to a better social good.

It's very difficult to say anything in general terms, because the discrepancies worldwide are so gigantic. In terms of the treatment of indigenous populations, we have moved from a kind of benign neglect — they will either integrate in the long-term or the problem will look after itself, this kind of benign neglect — to the real challenge of whether we are serious about empowering others who are basically claiming something we have — our land, for instance. That's where our rhetoric of equality and inclusion is very severely challenged.

And that, at the end of the day, is what we are supposed to be talking about when we talk about equality. It's the willingness to share wealth, to share power, and to articulate it as a matter of right and entitlement, which will imply surrendering something we already have. I think it's the same thing with men in power: it's the idea of surrendering part of their control over the exercise of power or the use of wealth, sharing that, given the idea that there's only so much around, right? We're not going to create new forms of power to accommodate the desire of women, for instance, to be part of it. So there's something you need to surrender, and I think that's where the rhetoric yields to, frankly, a less admirable reality.

~ FROM THE LECTURES

"I want to ask you … perhaps somewhat provocatively — if we have done everything within our power to give effect to those values, and those legal commitments, in our day-to-day life as a nation." **LOUISE ARBOUR**

"A questioning of certain myths that are suffocating Canada has therefore become necessary, in order that Canada embrace a nationalism that is positive and creative and that the country have at its disposal the tools it will need in the years that lie ahead." **ALAIN DUBUC**

"Nothing has happened over the past quarter century which has had an unredeemable, inevitable searing effect on our link to our past. On our ability to enforce our ethical standards. Or on the power of citizens to engage in responsible individualism. It is an insult to our intelligence and to the redeeming value of positive change to suggest that we are its passive victim, that it must dehumanize us and separate us from the reality of our ethics." **JOHN RALSTON SAUL**

"Why, despite our manifest commonality, do our differences, real and perceived, tend to define our world and dominate our discourse and our conduct?" BEVERLEY MCLACHLIN

"The greatest challenge to the world community in this century is how to promote harmonious relations between peoples of disparate origins, histories, languages and religions who find themselves intermingled in a single state." GEORGES ERASMUS

"Nothing defines a people more clearly than what they fear. Anxiety in your case springs from proximity — I'm sure I don't have to be more specific; ours from distance." DAVID MALOUF

"Canada suffers in many respects from the same ailments as Quebec. In fact, Canadian nationalism is also in the process of congealing under the weight of myths and dogmas that are becoming obstacles to the country's evolution." ALAIN DUBUC

"Canadians would probably ... agree in principle with the traditional Aboriginal ethic that our actions today should not jeopardize the health, peace and well-being of generations yet unborn." GEORGES ERASMUS

"The new idea of the equal worth of every person finds expression in the legal language of rights — human rights. If all people are equal, it follows that all people are equally entitled to freedom, fair treatment and respect. The rights are easily stated. The more difficult problem is to move them off the sterile page and into the reality of people's lives." BEVERLEY MCLACHLIN

"The possibility for people themselves to claim their human rights entitlements through legal processes is essential so that human rights have meaning for those most at the margins, a vindication of their equal worth and human agency." **LOUISE ARBOUR**

"Th[ese] moments when the temper of a society is defined and shown are decisive. It is these patterns of behaviour, this temper, more than any form of government that in the end determines the kind of society we create; how far it conforms to the common good; how, from one century to the next, it can be referred back to, and kept true to its own best self." **DAVID MALOUF**

"One of the hardest things to do in public policy is to marry ethics with effective programs. The cool arm's-length approach of ethics combined with simple, clear, all-inclusive policies can make that happen. And that would be an honest reflection of the trajectory that Louis LaFontaine and Robert Baldwin sent our way." **JOHN RALSTON SAUL**